MW00652878

THE CURIOUS VOYAGE

A RULE-BREAKING GUIDEBOOK TO AUTHENTICITY

CYNTHIA SCHWARTZBERG, LCSW

Copyright © 2021 by Cynthia Schwartzberg.

All rights reserved. No part of this publication may be reproduced, distributed or transmitted in any form or by any means, including photocopying, recording, or other electronic or mechanical methods, without the prior written permission of the publisher, except in the case of brief quotations embodied in critical reviews and certain other noncommercial uses permitted by copyright law. For permission requests, write to the publisher, addressed "Attention: Permissions Coordinator," at the email address below.

The author of this book does not dispense medical advice or prescribe the use of any technique as a form of treatment for physical, emotional or medical problems without the advice of a physician, either directly or indirectly. The intent of the author is only to offer information of a general nature to help you in your quest for emotional and spiritual well-being. In the event you use any of the information in this book for yourself, which is your constitutional right, the author and publisher assume no responsibility for your actions.

The events recounted in this manuscript are a compilation re-creating experiences with clients. The client presented is a representation of the work done by many individuals. Situations have been modified, expanded on or compressed. All names and identifying details have been changed for confidentiality purposes.

Cynthia Schwartzberg
info@cynthasis.com
www.cynthasis.com
Book Cover, Editing, and Layout ©2021 Stacey Ruth

Ordering Information:
Quantity sales. Special discounts are available on quantity purchases by corporations, associations and others. For details, contact the "Special Sales Department" at the email address above.

The Curious Voyage: A Rule-Breaking Guidebook to Authenticity/ Cynthia Schwartzberg. —1st ed.
ISBN 978-1-7371205-0-6 (Paperback)
ISBN 978-1-7371205-1-3 (eBook)

CONTENTS

Introduction 1

Chapter 1: The Journey to Connection 7

There's Always More to Know 8

Exercise 11

Our Connection to Humanity 13

Cultural Impact 17

Connection Is Essential 21

Power of Persuasion During Connection 22

We Are More Than Our Words and Thoughts 24

Connecting to the Body's Wisdom 29

More on Brain and Body Connection 30

Finding Your Inner Guide 33

Listening Within....................................... 33

Finding Your Answers 35

Exercises 36

Chapter 2: Becoming an Inner Explorer 45

Forming Beliefs 47

Moving Stuck Beliefs....................................48

Your Rulebook 49

Continuing to Find Your Inner Guide: Sifting Through Your
Rulebook 51

Our Mothers' Daughters and Our Fathers' Sons 55

You Be You 59

How Things Are Supposed To Be 60

Diving Deep 62

Culture, Faith, Religion 62

The Secret of Exploring 63

Stick With It and Pause 64

Exercises 65

Chapter 3: Redirecting Thoughts 75

Changing Your Mind... 75

You Can Direct Your Experience 78

The Four Colors 78

Saying Yes: Aligning With Desire 78

Intention and Decision... 79

You Always Have a Choice 81

Imagination... 82

Expectations 84

Radical Forgiveness: A Wide Lens of Understanding 88

Exercises 90

Chapter 4: Getting Curious About Energy and Love 107

Life Force.. 107

Breath.. 108

Choosing Love or Fear 109

Love and Compassion 111

Power 113

Connecting Power and Love..113

Serenity 114

Connecting to Serenity 116

Exercises 117

Chapter 5: Intuition and Receptivity 127

Intuition 127

Developing Intuition..129

Receptivity.. 130

Embracing Rhythm 133

Playing in the Universe 134

Exercise 134

Chapter 6: Destination Authenticity 137

Notes..139

ADDENDUM: EXERCISES 141

Chapter 1 Exercises..141

The Breath of Connection 141

Self-Spotting: Hearing the Body................................142

Connecting With Vibration: Exploring Your Currents 144

You Are Magnificent 146

Chapter 2 Exercises 148

Finding Beliefs 148

Priorities and Values 150

Back to Self.. 151

Washing Your Hands 152

Ball of Light: Cleansing Our Energy..............................153

Chapter 3 Exercises 156

Stuck Visions/Stuck Beliefs 156

Intention Setting 157

Receiving Positive Comments 158

Switching Little Voices 159

Meditation Using Three Voices..................................161

Start Digging Into What You Desire and Your Intention 166

Set Your Intentions..166

Visualization Into a New State 168

Nightly Gratitude 169

Clearing Pride, Self-will and Fear. 169

Chapter 4 Exercises 171

Love, Power, Serenity Exercise: Releasing Capes 171

Dancing Into Love 173

Brain/Body Connection Power 175

Breath to Connect Love and Power 176

Compassion 177

Chapter 5 Exercise...177

Listening 177

Dedicated to Jonathan Cohen,
who sat diligently supporting me every step of the way
and my daughter, Heather Schwartzberg,
for walking the path of healing with me.

I am deeply grateful to:
Life teachers including and not limited to:
Eva and John Pierrakos, MD, Diane Shainberg, PhD,
David Grand, PhD and Reverend David Ault.

Readers:
Drew Brazier, PsyD, Rosalie Chamberlain,
Shannon L. Dunn, Christine P. Leeds, LCSW,
Mark Seides, PhD, Lisa R. Terry, LPC,
Judy Van Dyke

And the many people who let me
witness their healing process.

If you obey all of the rules, you miss all of the fun.

—KATHARINE HEPBURN

INTRODUCTION

THERE IS AN OLD GREEK EXPRESSION, "Know thyself," which is followed by "Nothing to excess" and "Surety brings ruin."

If you are a seeker, feeling lost or confused, wanting deeper relationships and/or wanting greater peace and joy, this book can answer your call. We will be taking a voyage with stories and tools and discovering a state of presence, living in the moment with conviction and confidence—authenticity. This voyage will open doors to a state of aliveness, deep knowing, joy and peace.

How can we be authentic and know thyself with uncertainty? Putting these two thoughts together, I would say it is good to discover and know thyself to connect to a sense of authenticity.

How I understand myself one day may not be the way I understand myself the next. Yet, there are certain threads of self that remain. One thread is an inner voice of knowing. This voice has been referred to as soul, core self, higher power, God—to name a few references. Whatever it is called, it speaks with a wisdom that helps life flow more smoothly.

This book will strengthen your connection to your voice. It will direct you to a level of joy you may presently think is too hard to reach. You can reach it. I and hundreds of people I helped have walked this journey and have settled into a deep, peaceful inner joy. It is our birthright.

Over the years this inner voice got louder. My intention to trust and listen got stronger. One day in particular I remember it as a whisper I barely heard. We were headed to the beach, car packed, bikes chain-locked on a rack behind the car. Off we went, and then it was time to stop for gas. Getting out of the car I had locked the bike lock and put the key in my pocket. The whisper spoke: "Don't do that." I did it. The key went into my pocket, so I thought. Finally, we arrived at the beach. It was time to unlock the bikes, but I had no key. Mind you, this lock was too complex for the locksmith who had to direct me to a chicken farmer who was a welder. The farmer removed the chain.

From the moment I noticed there was no key, I was angry. I looked forward to biking on the beach all year. I felt upset, embarrassed, mad at myself. The whole range of disappointment flooded me. It took hours for me to relax and enjoy the beach. "If I only listened," was one key phrase coursing through me. Were all those feelings my authentic self, or was this one of those golden opportunities to dive deeper to know thyself? This experience returns to me many times as an example of listening and not listening to that inner voice. We will dive into examples like this to gain tools on listening and knowing thyself.

Recently I was cleaning out the garage desiring to give our roller blades away but not knowing to whom. We were in the middle of being quarantined at home so options of seeing people were limited. As I was cleaning the inner voice said, "Put them at the end of the driveway now." I listened. A mother and son were on an Easter egg hunt. Something inspired me to say, "Hey, would you like some roller blades?" They were surprised and happy to say "yes." It ended up the mother wore the size of one pair and the son the size of the other. That night my heart was filled with gratitude to know I made a difference. It was mutual. I listened, they had a wonderful Easter egg hunt, and I felt joy.

What helped me develop the connection to this inner voice is what I would like to share with you. This guidebook is designed to give you tools and stories to help you dive deeper into your own feelings, thoughts and actions. It will lead you from the self-questions of what beliefs are mine, what have I been taught along the way, what is the life that I choose to live and what creative expression is bursting to be born and expressed. It does not matter what your profession is. This is not about a career. It's about a way of living to your fullest potential and feeling content and happy as you connect deeper to yourself, others, community and that which you may call God.

It was a process and a practice that I have developed over the years from all the experiences I have had with my personal development and with the journey of helping hundreds of others.

I have longed to understand myself and others the bulk of my life. As a child I was curious about life and wanted to serve others—but wondered how. In college I gained tools to fulfill this longing from the Pathwork teachings. These teachings gave me a foundation for a perspective that helped me grow and develop myself as a human being. I am deeply grateful for having discovered them so long ago. I worked hard applying the teachings to my life and later being trained to support others on their life journey. I thought that as a professional I needed more education to help those on various paths. Each of us needs to find a language that speaks to our authentic self so we can connect and get curious about what matters to our heart. The language we discover rings a bell to an inner calling we have. It is a natural human condition to seek growth. If you are reading this book, I gather that longing is within you too.

One key take away is that evolution has many beginnings, middles and endings. As a seeker I have gathered many tools on my journey that have helped me and others uncover a more comfortable way of living that feels true to our nature. I am offering this guidebook as a resource to help you navigate unknown waters within to find deeper levels, discover talents you did not know you had, and find a connection to something greater than what you thought you were supposed to be.

This book will guide you to living beyond the "supposed to's" and living a creative life no matter what your outer vocation may be. It is set up as a voyage. You are the Captain of your Ship of Life. How you chart the course has to do with how you experience life. May this book help you explore the way you have been steering your ship and guide you to waters that flow well with who you innately are. Throughout this voyage you will be evaluating the rulebook of your life. Our rulebook is made up of the things we were taught, our family, community and society at large, traditions, ways we were taught to treat people, values, priorities, and collective attitudes and beliefs. This book suggests you get to know how you respond to life on automatic pilot and may be going against your personal truth and authentic self. You are guided to become aware, evaluate, edit and in some cases re-write your book. We will discover, as we follow our hearts, our true nature with love and care for all living beings, that we do not need to have rules. We connect to a deeper truth that is beyond all rules. Enjoy the journey.

[1]

THE JOURNEY TO CONNECTION

LIKE ANY SELF-RESPECTING REBEL, I am known to break the rules often. Rule breaking is not an act of defiance or violence. It is an act of the deepest allegiance to our own truth. This truth is in our DNA. Mine is a quieter, more introspective rebellion. When culture and authority tell me how to spend my time, I resist. I have always known there is so much more than following someone else's idea of how I live my life. That's the only place I know to grow—from following my own inner compass.

This inner discovery has provided me with amazing awareness that might seem strange to many readers. While others were out playing sports and video games, I went within. Even as a child, I was aware of my own transformations, especially where emotion and connections were concerned.

At the end of sixth grade, walking up the hill on my way home, I was listening to the transistor radio, and memories of the year flooded in. The music brought up a particular friendship that year with two other girls that did not get along with one another. Traveling as I did, to a different drummer, I had managed to stay friends with both by treating each one with respect and kindness, rather than picking sides. The trust I created meant the world to all three of us. It was an early discovery of the powerful energy connection we can create with others and also create within ourself.

When I entered junior high school, I read the Bible with a friend. As a result, we had long conversations about life and death. I became curious about what happens when you die and started drifting into thoughts of wishing I could die—just to find out! Thank goodness, my wise inner voice let me know that was not possible! At the time my parents were divorcing, and it was no coincidence that I became curious about death as their marriage was dying.

My parents had the insight for us to all see a therapist to navigate the loss and change in our family dynamic. That therapeutic experience was a pivotal one for me. In the safety of her office, I came to understand that my inner world was as valid and meaningful as anyone else's outer world. My rebellion was affirmed as worthwhile.

I knew then that I wanted to help people like me—the rebels and the rulebreakers who want to understand more about the world. I felt a calling to connect at a deeper level with myself and others—a calling that many people are not fully aware of. A seed was planted for me then.

There's Always More to Know

My early internal, non-judgmental inquiry about life was soon swallowed up in worries about paying bills and nagging doubts that there was something wrong with me. Unfortunately, that is not uncommon. It took me many years and some very painful experiences to re-learn what I had known as a girl— there was nothing wrong with me. I was living out of the box and into my truth. Now I know an even bigger truth—there is no box! Following our heart and our truth is the only "rule" we need.

During this often-bumpy journey of self-rediscovery, I learned none of us can avoid every rule. Rules, guidelines and norms inevitably come from our family, culture and conditions growing up. They shape who we know ourselves to be. Still, when they don't line up with our inner truth, the result is painful.

I have had countless people come to me for therapy because of that pain when they felt challenged by situations at work and in relationships. Frequently, people in their lives are not behaving the way they want. They feel misunderstood, invisible and rejected. Often their pain comes from feeling stuck, making poor choices and repeating painful patterns in relationships, struggling with money, creativity or health issues. This is an almost universal experience.

When I focus with these patients on their beliefs first—whether they are personal, religious or cultural beliefs—a natural inner state of peace, love and fully expressed life rises up in them. Exploring true and false beliefs of my own is something I continue to do. There is always something new to discover and greater personal peace to experience. Getting curious and seeking what the truth is creates a lot of energy and freedom. I invite you to travel this journey to expand your current relationships and enhance your life.

This is a guidebook designed for you to read with curiosity. It will take you on a voyage of self-discovery, where each chapter is full of useful exercises. By taking the time to explore each exercise, you will be able to unpack old ideas and beliefs that you no longer want to carry in the ship of your own life and cast them overboard. The exercises are designed to bring you into an expanded feeling of presence, love, joy and authenticity.

On this voyage we will take together, I suggest you pack a journal to record your progress, as there are plenty of writing exercises. Writing is a brilliant tool of self-discovery, whether you use paper, computer or voice memo. Putting down your thoughts on paper can help shift and move them beyond what you're thinking. Writing can also shift your energy.

It might seem extreme, but the exercises are not to be done while driving, operating machinery or doing any activity that requires focused attention. Much of the work is meditative. Other activities may either distract you from the work, or the work may distract you from your activities.

The best way to experience a sense of connection is to find it within ourselves. As children, we may have immersed ourselves in creative play and daydreaming. We may think nothing of staring, looking and wondering. I remember one childhood day sitting on a dock, oblivious to time passing, just staring at a motorboat gliding across the lake. I sat in that stillness, curiosity and wonder for what might have been moments or hours. In that bubble, I could hear someone call my name, but there was no one around. I felt it was the state of wonder calling. Our life is meant to be a voyage filled with adventure and wonder. We don't have to understand where the voice is coming from. We only need to hear the call and follow something larger than ourselves.

I invite you to enter your Ship of Life, pack your gear and steer through the charted path contained in this guidebook. If you commit to doing the work here, you can find your own calling, stillness and freedom. Let's start with an exercise that generates a timeless, wonder-filled feeling of connection.

EXERCISE:

THE BREATH OF CONNECTION

1. Take a few deep breaths and get settled into a sitting position you can be comfortable in for five minutes. You may want to add some gentle music to this process.

2. As you breathe in and out, consider the air you are breathing is made up of atoms that have been around for thousands of years. Now consider this same air is part of what others are also inhaling and exhaling. The air is made of atoms that move around the Earth's atmosphere.

3. Continue to bring your awareness into your breath. Consider each breath is part of a larger atmosphere stretching beyond what you can sense.

4. Now, shift your awareness to your heart. As you feel it pumping blood throughout your body, consider the blood is made up mostly of water. The water surging through you right now is made of atoms that have been on the planet for centuries. These atoms in your blood contain hydrogen from an infinite universe and oxygen from the stars.

5. Experiencing this connection to the atoms, keep your awareness in your heart, and begin to imagine a yellow ribbon of light flowing out from your heart to the heart of someone you know. Imagine the ribbon then flowing out from that person's heart to someone else you both know. The ribbon continues on to someone that those two people know and then to someone you may not know but who lives in the neighborhood. This ribbon of light continues to flow, connecting to still others, multiplying connections, all the way around the globe.

6. You may not know all these individuals, but in this moment, consider how you are all connected. Keep breathing in and out, contemplating this sense of connection.

7. When you are ready, take out a journal/electronic note and write a little about your experience.

Although we may feel this state of connection from time to time, we often lose our awareness of it. Daily demands and habits interfere. However, as we dive into the topic of connection, taking the time to set aside the demands and habits that block us, we discover our authentic self, creativity and love.

This book will offer several opportunities to peel back some of your conditioning so you can uncover something fresh for yourself. I will refer to this conditioning as "rules," and we will work on writing the Book of Life you want to live without trying to please, predict, anticipate or fear others.

Let's turn to wonder—wondering how we got here and what our purpose is.

Our Connection to Humanity

We are connected to each other through the air we breathe, our skin, and the space between every other person we know and us. At this first stop on our voyage, we are getting curious about our connection to one another and the impact we have on every life we touch. We will see how each of us embodying this connection seriously and acting in accordance with it can make a difference in our own life too. Each choice we make creates a ripple in humanity. You matter, and your actions create the world we all live in together.

Some say we are stardust, made up of atoms shared by other galaxies. Others suggest we come from God or originate from the Big Bang. Whatever theory you choose, there's no arguing we are here! However, if you are a bit like me, you want something more. You desire meaning and purpose in your life. It's in our nature to want those things. Let's sail over to discovering what those are for you.

We will start our quest for purpose and meaning at the beginning of time, steering through the places where we are all connected and navigate the newer frontiers in science, where we exist as electrical fields. We will be re-mapping the rules we have been living by and finding what we desire for our lives. I will provide the necessary support to help you shift into your greatest self with your own vital personal expression.

Science teaches us a tremendous amount about how we got here, but it also can raise as many questions as it does answers. For instance, evolution teaches us that we evolved from the oldest human, Lucy, who lived 3.2 million years ago. Evolutionary theory is built on the idea that all life on Earth is connected and related to each other. In other words, life diversity is a result of natural selection shifts in the DNA of living things, where certain characteristics are preferred over others in an environment.

Given how different we are today from Lucy via the constant process of evolution, we can almost see the evolution we are undergoing right now. Still, much of our current evolution is invisible. It's happening in our minds first. There is growing information about how our thoughts impact our bodies and our behavior. Studies of the brain and neuroplasticity show we actually change our physical brains by how we think. Neural pathways can grow and reorganize based on our thoughts.

This is what it means to be human. It is our birthright, handed down from Lucy. How we think will have an evolutionary impact on future generations. That is only the beginning. Bruce Lipton, in his work, *The Biology of Belief*, tells us that each cell in our body is a universe by itself. He vividly describes how a cell's genes are like a computer's hard drive, and "every cell can form any kind of cell because every nucleus has all the genes that make up a human."[1]

According to Lipton, our external environment constantly provides information to each cell in our bodies and impacts how the cell will function. Comparing our body to a garden, if a cell nucleus was a bag full of various seeds, we could plant any seed we wish. He is suggesting we can change ourselves at a cellular level.

Beliefs are akin to seeds we plant into the soil of our subconscious. I can change the seed to something else to get a different plant. But even after I plant it, I still need to water my garden and weed out whatever is popping up and crowding out the plant I want to grow. I also need to be patient. Plants grow over time.

Some of us may find that hard to believe. The important point here is that numerous scientific studies across a diverse set of disciplines are beginning to line up behind the idea that what we think has a direct, measurable impact on our physical experience.

PAUSE: *What we think has a direct, measurable impact on our physical experience.*

I admit I have experimented with altering how my body operates—from metabolism to the common cold—but discovered it is actually a process—not an event. What's more, it is a collaborative process with something bigger than simply my willing it to be so. Some things change faster than others. Much like a computer, some software programs have other hidden operations, and we need to address the hidden programs first before reprogramming the entire system.

I had an experience with hidden beliefs in myself when I saw the Broadway show *Baby*. It was about three couples trying to get pregnant. There was one couple who could not get pregnant. Something in that moment hit me close to home, which I did not understand at the time. Later I questioned if I planted that seed or was that striking a chord in me because I knew that was my path. This is where these things can be tricky. Our conscious mind is not the only part of us that is at play here. Life involves other people and their journey. We are all interconnected. Also, what we feel we want may not be what we really want. Perhaps a part of me really wanted to adopt, so I could mother the child I ultimately did. I am very grateful today for how things did not turn out like I once thought they should. In my experience too much analysis can lead to paralysis.

One mental seed that grew into a weed for me was back pain. However, I was able to shift it with curiosity.

One day I woke up with back pain and thought, *How is it I can help other people and not help myself?* The pain was intense and unforgiving. I could not dismiss it. Thankfully, I was able to perform a healing process on myself called Self-Spotting. I will share more about this incredible process later. For now, though, I was able to become deeply curious about the pain.

I focused on it and realized it began the night before, dancing with my dance teacher. As we were dancing, I started second-guessing myself, wondering, *What does he want me to do?* I felt unable to anticipate what was coming next. This was an old, familiar thought for me. Once this came to my awareness, I started laughing at myself. I remembered countless times I wondered that same question to myself, trying to figure out what a man wanted me to do. My dancing was no longer fluid when my mind wandered into my rulebook of pleasing the man. Not only that, it caused me some serious injury.

I was brought up with the concept of supporting the man and not standing out as a separate person. By shifting into thought and out of the moment, I was hurt. Once I connected my body pain and the thinking behind it, there was a release in my back and the pain left! The idea had been the root cause of my injury—not my physical body!

This is an example of how the brain and body connection can relieve our pains as we get curious and discover the interrelationship that may be rooted in our rulebook. Through awareness, curiosity and digging into the dirt of my rulebook, beliefs and life situations changed for the better. Whether they changed me at the level of my DNA has yet to be seen.

> PAUSE: Get curious about the beliefs/seeds you plant based on your rulebook.

CULTURAL IMPACT

How we function as individuals is impacted by our culture. We are taught ways to think, behave and function based on the society, socioeconomic and political environment in which we grew up. Those beliefs, nonetheless, do come with a built-in choice as we grow up. We can continue to believe them or change them for a fresh set of beliefs. Every thought and belief we have within us will impact the way we show up in the world and the kind of world we create for ourselves. The inside is connected to the outside, and the outside is connected to the inside.

We can't change the experiences we have, but we can influence our relationship to them. So, if our beliefs are strong enough to shift our brains, and in turn that shifts our experiences, it may be possible to have a stronger influence on our outside world than we realized. At the end of Chapter 3, there are exercises to help dig into your own beliefs and shift them.

Where do I actually stop and start?

We have looked at connection and how it affects us all. In connection, there is an interrelationship between people and between all of existence, down to a cellular level. Considering life at all levels will help us realize that every thought and every action we make influences existence in multiple ways.

As we move further into our journey, we will see how to re-map our rulebook and shape our experiences.

The other day I received a thank you letter from a student describing how I helped change her life. This shift was the result of a series of events that happened without us ever speaking. I was helping someone during a Brainspotting workshop demonstration, and she was watching my face during the work. Just seeing me helped her make her own connections internally and healed a long-standing problem she was having. That workshop led to shifting many lives way beyond my awareness at the time.

> PAUSE: *Think of the decisions in your life that had a ripple effect on others.*

Our decisions impact the lives around us as well as within us, especially within our bodies. Everything in life is connected down to the atomic level. Everything is energy. Not only do particles consist of energy, but so does the space between them. As we go on this voyage, we will discover the capacity of our own creativity. As a result, we can learn to work with our bodies and consciousness at the level of these basic building blocks of existence.

Consider one of our bodies' key building blocks, a cell, and look at its border. The membrane of a cell is semipermeable, meaning things go in and out all the time. As a result, there is no concrete wall stopping something from inside the cell from being connected to something outside of it. The cell brilliantly selects what goes in and what stays out. Our bodies' cells expand to connect with other cells as they create the different parts of our body. Each part works together in an interconnection to help us move and function. Our cells have a mind of their own, it would seem.

We can learn from these cells when it comes to interacting with our thoughts and with others. We do not have to take in everything we hear. Instead, we can select what goes in and what stays out. I can hear someone, I can feel compassion and love, but their challenges and behaviors do not have to become mine. I do not have to change my value system because of another's. Even so, I can choose to connect with others in community to create something bigger than myself. We are all an integral part of the whole of life.

I think of this interconnection when I sit with clients. They are not really separate or disconnected from me. These people are my fellow humans seeking support with something they have not been able to resolve on their own. Sitting with someone, and realizing we are all connected, changes the dynamic of any relationship. This is especially true when I am not taking on their troubles as my own. I sit with them, hearing their pain or frustration, and desire to help them find a path out. This is a state of compassion.

In truth, any person we engage with carries infinite connections, including their present family, community, culture and society at large. It reminds me of the 6-degrees of separation, the concept that all people are six or fewer social connections away from each other. When we look at this larger perspective, it further enhances the reason why we need to do our work.

In the larger perspective, it is unavoidable that we are all connected.

There are many levels of connections from the cellular level to the atomic level to the molecules of the air we breathe. All living things share the same air—other humans, plants, cats, dogs, and birds. Ralph Keeling, professor at the Scripps Institution of Oceanography and the Principal Investigator for the Atmospheric Oxygen Research Group, puts it this way, "Oxygen gas emitted by plants and plankton mixes throughout each respective hemisphere within two months and spreads worldwide in a little more than a year. The sensitivity of the oxygen and carbon dioxide balance of the atmosphere to the activities of living things shows that recycling is not just a passing fad but a tradition that has always been practiced on the atomic level by all life on Earth."[2]

Our connection to each other is nearer and more real than we might have imagined. The saying, "Nothing belongs to us. Not even the air we breathe," should be re-written to say it belongs to us all, equally. This reminds me of when I was at a workshop and the teacher was speaking about this theory of breathing in the air of others and being connected. My mind wandered to thinking,

So if I turn my head because I don't like someone's smell, you are telling me whether I like it or not, it is a part of me.

The COVID-19 pandemic makes this concept very immediate and real. During this time, we have been staying in our homes and away from each other because the COVID-19 virus moves through air and directly impacts our respiratory system. No one on the planet can avoid it. This deep uncertainty of knowing what is actually in the air is nothing new, except now we see its effects. You may be reading this long after COVID-19, but know it may be something else. We can't escape our deep connection to one another.

CONNECTION IS ESSENTIAL

PAUSE: We need connection to survive. As social creatures, we are wired to be connected.

Social interaction and bonding are necessary for our survival. It starts at birth. Harry Harlow's classic behavioral studies with primates show that without bonding from the beginning, we perish. Since then, evidence has piled up in support of the critical importance connection has on our well-being.

Studies have also shown the benefits of social engagement with aging. The findings suggest social connecting may actually preserve the part of our brain associated with memory known as the hippocampus. Normally the hippocampus diminishes with age. Social engagement, mental and physical exercise all help with memory. These studies add to our reasons for social engagement.

In addition, scientist Michael Lieberman explained the neuroscience of human connections and the broad implications for how we live our lives in *Scientific American*:

"Evolution has placed a bet that the best thing for our brain to do in any spare moment is to get ready to see the world socially. I think that makes a major statement about the extent to which we are built to be social creatures."[3]

One great way to connect is through the act of giving. Research done by Elizabeth Dunn and Michael Norton points to the connection between giving and happiness. When we give to others, we are happier. Giving directly affects the pleasure center of our brain.

POWER OF PERSUASION DURING CONNECTION

Across many studies of mammals, from the smallest rodents to humans, the data suggests that our social environment profoundly shapes us and that we suffer greatly when our social bonds are threatened or severed. When this happens in childhood, it can lead to long-term health and educational problems.[3]

We can't avoid connection. The same connection that defines our survival also disconnects us from our true selves. Society's messages can be so strong that we forget the difference between what we are thinking and what society tells us to think. Studies show we are highly influenced by signage, constant news, teachers, parents, friends, neighbors, relatives and even our lineage. It is all part of our subconscious. Jung refers to some of these deep influences as the collective unconscious.

The influence of culture can persuade us to veer from our authentic selves without realizing it. However, there are times, such as COVID-19, where the world provides us a window where we are able to assess our essential need for connection and the norms of our cultural habits.

Social engagement, including communication, has its pros and cons. Persuasion can lead us away from our true values and priorities without realizing it. Studies on persuasion show that the same parts of our brain engaged with persuasion are where we register information about our social network. Lieberman says, "Rather than being a hermetically sealed vault that separates us from others, our research suggests that the self is more of a Trojan horse, letting in the beliefs of others, under the cover of darkness, and without us realizing it."[3]

My mother was very persuasive—especially when it came to me. Years ago, I was looking for a house. She happened to be with me when I needed to stop in and check on something at the new residence. Knowing how she could sway me, I pre-emptively warned her, "Don't tell me anything about how you do or don't like things!"

Like many of us, I was aware that any comment from her could alter my feelings about this new place I was really excited about. I did not feel strong enough to withstand a different opinion from her. She could so easily get under my skin. It took time to develop that strong, trusting sense of my own self, separate and equally valid, from hers.

PAUSE: Who has been getting under your skin and persuading you lately?

WE ARE MORE THAN OUR WORDS AND THOUGHTS

To understand ourselves beyond words and thoughts, try to visualize yourself as made of electrical currents. It's not such a stretch. Humans have electricity running through their bodies all the time. Our brains actually have enough electrical current to power a 15- to 20-watt light bulb. The heart transmits the electrical charge to contract in one coordinated motion, creating a heartbeat. We also each emit enough electrical current to impact another person's energy. Have you ever been in a crowd or around another individual and felt drained or energized for no reason? If so, then you'll understand when I say humans can absorb and emit electrical currents creating an electrical field beyond their physical body.

Now let's think of the surface of our body—our skin. As I said before, my mother's statements easily got under my skin. Although this is a metaphor, there is truth to the fact that my skin is porous and the electrical currents in my body are in constant motion.

Science has explained our bodies are not solid.[4] The electrical currents we are made of are a flow of electrons through a complete circuit of our bodies. While I am standing close to people, I can feel them. I may feel a desire to get closer or to pull away. It is all subcortical that I can't always know the reasons why I feel that way. It is part of our system to sense, feel and respond.

We have seen our connection through air. Now we are seeing how we are connected through our bodies. As discussed earlier, Bruce Lipton spoke of how we can change our experience based on how we relate to our outer environment. Let's consider that one main way we relate to our outer environment is by how we interpret it and think about it—our thoughts.

Another connection to explore is the electrical charge of our thoughts. Our thoughts are made of neurons in our brains. Donald Hebb in 1949 stated, "Neurons that fire together wire together." Meaning our neurons that connect with electrical currents called synaptic connections will develop neuropathways. It is becoming understood that over time these become set thoughts. As we change our thoughts that, in a sense, have become habitual patterns, we can change our neurons that are wired together.

Current technologies have proved either too broad or too specific to track how tiny amounts of neurotransmitters in and around many cells might contribute to the transmission of a thought. Scientists have used functional magnetic resonance imaging to look at blood flow as a surrogate for brain activity over fairly long periods of time or have employed tracers to follow the release of a particular neurotransmitter from a small set of neurons for a few seconds.[5]

One day I saw this in action. David Grand, PhD and I went to a university lab to see how Brainspotting works in the brain. He gave me a session while in an fMRI machine. This one subject experiment revealed information that was later used to support the articles on how Brainspotting works.[6]

Brainspotting, developed by David Grand, PhD in 2003, is based on the idea that "where you look affects how you feel." If you are feeling upset about your pain, and look in one direction you will experience it differently than when you look in another direction.

As an example, Sharon came to me with a tightness in her chest causing breathing problems. We had already worked for a little over a year on various other issues such as: challenging family relationships, trouble sleeping and school bullying. By the time the chest problem came up, she was already feeling a stronger connection to herself as a unique, creative, smart and talented individual. Her realization that her brain functioned differently helped her accept her uniqueness.

However, she was still struggling with chest pain. In a Brainspotting session, Sharon brought her attention to her chest. She spent some time being curious about the pain, feeling into her chest and entire torso area while gazing at a spot that helped her connect to the pain. This activity of looking and connecting to the pain, brought up feelings of being empty and lonely. Far from staying stuck in those feelings, after about ten minutes of this focused mindfulness process, she felt relief.

Not only did this help create a deep healing of both the pain and the emotions, the healing was so transformative that it freed up Sharon's creativity to write a play about her experience!

Although we may not all be able to go home, write a play and get it produced after a single session, this is a testament to the power of Brainspotting. It is important to note that we each have our individual timing and personal approach that works best.

Focused attention to our body's sensations is a great way to discover key beliefs and feelings. This creates the possibility for healing to emerge as we sort through the beliefs from our rulebook and the inner wisdom that comes in quiet moments of going within.

> PAUSE: *Connecting to our body's sensations is a great way to discover and release energy, sensations or pain—as well as connect to key beliefs and feelings.*

The Self-Spotting Exercise at the end of this chapter can give you an opportunity to try Brainspotting. You may experience a shift as Sharon did while you sit with a body sensation, then take a deep breath and notice a release of tension. Shifts sometimes come in making a connection to two seemingly unrelated thoughts. Other times, you may experience a gradual shift from being very upset about an issue to feeling calm without a conscious connection.

Another example of Brainspotting, which shows how our thoughts and bodies can work together in our healing, is with Claire. Claire is a well-dressed, middle-aged woman. She came and reported, "I am a mess. I have been in therapy for years and have no idea how you can help, but I am willing to try." The key in her statement was the admission of willingness to be helped. That's how I knew I could help her. There is so much truth in the adage, "Where there is a will, there is a way." Claire had the will to come to therapy and the desire to heal her "mess," as she put it. That is what we all need as the first step in any journey—the desire. We need to connect to a part inside us that says, "I don't want to go on like this anymore. I want something to change." We will look closer at the inner voice that directs us later in this chapter.

Claire's journey was a winding road, full of twists and turns. As we worked together, she shared various challenges such as the loss of a close cousin, the need to move, being robbed, losing her job, and being mistreated in intimate relationships. As we explored her story, she noticed the pattern of events in her life were connected to low self-esteem. She had repeatedly been willing to put up with people who had demonstrated they were not to be trusted. She eventually began to realize that she could choose to take control of her habits in thinking and behavior.

With the help of the tools mentioned throughout the book and Brainspotting, Claire began to challenge her own negative thought patterns, and she also started to take better care of her health. Although making fresh choices is still a challenge for her in many areas, she is committed to the process and has created a smoother, more direct path. Already she is seeing positive change, realizing inner strength beyond what she thought possible and developing new relationships.

This transformation that Claire created for herself took her from a self-proclaimed mess, doubtful she could change, to an empowered, self-actualized woman. As she courageously sorted through her life's traumas, she realized not only did those experiences not define who she was, but neither did her beliefs about herself resulting from them. The Brainspotting helped her experience her body's innate wisdom to heal itself.

Claire came to recognize she was the Captain of her own life's ship, and she was ready to steer it. You can do it too. Ultimately, we are each the Captain of our own ship. We can connect to that desire and start to put action behind it. One way of putting that action behind our desire is simply to follow the exercises laid out in this book. The exercises clarify how you have been thinking about things, give tools to shift your thoughts and your own energetic patterns, and help you embrace a new way of being.

Of course, a new way of being doesn't generally happen overnight. Give yourself time to contemplate each concept, and try the suggestions. The following sections will include things for your body, mind and heart. Let's see how we can sail our ship and discover not only a world that is not flat but one that is beyond 3D!

CONNECTING TO THE BODY'S WISDOM

Claire learned that the body pain she had experienced was another effect of her traumatic experiences. As she started the road to healing, she began to treat herself differently, managing her body pain with more awareness and kinder attention. Naturally, not all pain is connected to emotional trauma. It can arise from illness, sports injuries, car accidents, or even poor diet, repetitive movements or bad posture. Whatever the source, our bodies talk to us, and the more we are connected and willing to listen, the more embodied we become.

As you explore later examples and exercises, you will realize that you have an opportunity to make a difference immediately. I encourage you to go beyond the obvious thoughts, such as, *Oh, this is interesting.* Don't let yourself just stop there. Here is a chance to invest in yourself. You deserve it! Consider this as an experiment: exploring you, learning and discovering unexpected possibilities.

MORE ON BRAIN AND BODY CONNECTION

We already discussed our connection to other people. In the examples of Sharon and Claire, we looked at the connection of body and mind. Now, let's get more curious about our bodies.

It is through our bodies that we experience the world. The body is filled with electrical signals, and as with anything conducting electricity, we need to be grounded. We ground with our bodies through contact and connection. For a grounding exercise, you may go to my website: https://www.cynthasis.com/the-curious-voyage-resources/. Additionally, there are numerous other grounding exercises on YouTube.

Still, sometimes our bodies are so ungrounded we need therapy to relieve stress, tension and dysregulation. People come to therapy when it has become hard to reset, and they find themselves withdrawn, fighting a lot, giving more than they want or finding no relief from physical symptoms despite intervention/consultation with medical doctors. In a supportive therapeutic relationship, we can sort out the past from the present and become regulated in present time. When a present situation reminds us of the past, we automatically move and behave as we did in the past, without thinking. Working with our brain/body connection helps us shift from unconscious, emotional reactions to becoming more present and conscious.

Damir del Monte, a German therapist and brain researcher, proposed that in order for therapy to be effective we need to activate the self-regulatory system in the brain. In other words, no amount of talk therapy and analysis can impact how our body holds kinetic memories of reacting and responding in self-protection. We literally hold physical memories of survival—real or perceived.

Claire was a perfect example of this. She had repeated painful relationship patterns based on her trauma history. All the intellectual understanding in the world could not stop her from repeating the same pattern in her next relationship. However, Claire was fortunate that Brainspotting helped her shift her physical survival instincts.

Brainspotting helped Claire understand her issues from a brain body perspective rather than from the negative beliefs she was carrying about herself. So often, we think something is wrong with our personhood when it is really a problem in our brain based on trauma. David Grand, PhD, says that Brainspotting is a physiological approach with psychological consequences. We may not know which comes first, like the chicken or the egg. But what we do know is, as we help the brain and body regulate and work to full capacity, we can discover our greatness beyond any rulebook.

PAUSE: As we help the brain and body regulate and work to full capacity, we can discover our own greatness beyond any rulebook.

We all have our days or moments of being upset, which often arise because we do not feel safe. In those moments, we often automatically respond in a self-protective manner. Over time, that style of self-protection can lead to stomach aches, back pain, short temper or feeling disconnected. Do you ever say, "No," before you realized what was asked of you? Or do you tighten your body to run or fight because something felt inexplicably threatening? These natural reactions are survival instincts that happen so fast we don't even think about it.

Another modality that connects the brain and body is B.R.E.T.H. work (Breath Releasing Energy for Transformation and Healing). B.R.E.T.H. work is a healing process that helps someone release a negative belief. As a B.R.E.T.H. participant, you pick a belief you want to change and then sit with a partner who supports you while you lie down and breathe to music, which often includes a heartbeat sound.

During the time you are breathing, you experience various sensations and images. B.R.E.T.H. work experiences are as individual as the person—as are the results. Some people laugh, while others cry. Some feel hot, while others feel cold. Other sensations include tingling, pressure, floating and heaviness. As a result, the only thing to expect is the unexpected. Still, it is intended to be safe and supportive. The person sitting with you holds their arms to support you, no matter what you feel.

Once during B.R.E.T.H. work, my body went into a posture where my backside was trying to push, and then my feet started to kick. The facilitator remarked that I was probably a breach birth. Later I spoke to my mother, and she told me that was absolutely correct—which was news to me—but obviously, my body remembered what my mind could not. The body never lies.

That experience showed me quite vividly how I got here physically. It also gave me a more expansive idea about myself and who I thought I was. B.R.E.T.H. work has taken me to spiritual experiences beyond the physical. I can only describe it as my soul opening and connecting in ways I could not have experienced otherwise.

I shifted from an awareness and understanding of myself into a knowing of myself, because I embodied my experiences. I learned the body is a vital part of feeling connected. It is also the gateway to our authentic self. All parts of us create our uniqueness, guiding us to our inner wisdom. Let's now see how to strengthen the connection to our inner wisdom.

FINDING YOUR INNER GUIDE

Together we have explored the impact society has on our individual rulebook. We have delved into the body and brain connection. Still, there is more to know by going deeper within and listening to what is waiting for us there. It's here we can gain clarity about our beliefs, what our bodies are telling us, our choices and our creativity.

LISTENING WITHIN

Listening within strengthens our connection to our heart and our authentic self. It helps us question the beliefs of our culture.

Life is filled with unanswered questions. Nobody has the answers for us more than we do. We need to reassess the external influences on our rulebook and listen within to live more authentically.

You may feel uncomfortable sitting in the unknown of your inner world—yet you are never alone. There is a voice that is always there. This voice is beyond the effects of the outer influences on our rulebook—our culture, upbringing, heredity, as well as various disciplines such as science, medicine, psychology, and theology. All the information we gather from outside of ourselves can't fully give us the answer that is right for us. We need to decide for ourselves.

In former President Barack Obama's words: "All those adults that you used to think were in charge and knew what they were doing? Turns out that they don't have all the answers. A lot of them aren't even asking the right questions. So, if the world's going to get better, it's going to be up to you. Listen to the truth that's inside yourself—even when it's hard, even when it's inconvenient, people will notice. They'll gravitate toward you. And you'll be part of the solution instead of part of the problem."[7]

> *PAUSE: Have you ever been faced with a decision about what is right for you, gathered opinions and information then went with a gut feeling?*

Daily intuitive answers come more readily when we are comfortable in our own skin and listen within, trusting in ourselves. That takes time and experience. We may need to ask a question of ourselves repeatedly before we get real clarity. If you don't have the answer right away, wait and it will come. Inner knowing can't be forced. I have experience letting myself live with the question until something comes into awareness. It may come from comments someone makes in a conversation or through hearing two or more people mention the exact same idea that leads you to the answer. Sometimes I will sit with the question in meditation with great curiosity and let go of the need to get an answer. That is exactly when the answer arises. In

Chapter 3, we look more at expectations. Sitting with curiosity, we learn to trust, believe, and feel a sense of self. We feel more fully connected.

As a therapist, I am constantly afforded opportunities to recognize that I don't have other people's answers for them. I cannot know a client by their diagnosis or by what another professional says. Instead, I need to meet them, see them in the present moment and help them with support and tools that have proven to work time after time. This is how I can provide a supportive space for them to discover their own unique answers, listen to their inner voice and find hope. That's what this book is all about— getting more and more curious to find your own answers— from within.

FINDING YOUR ANSWERS

A teacher once told me that if I have the question, then I have the answer. I sit with clients trusting their innate wisdom to heal themselves. You can do this too.

It is a fine balance between realizing I have the answer within and yet what I know is—I know nothing. This balance between wisdom, curiosity and uncertainty is what makes life really interesting. As we re-map our rulebook under the guidance of our inner voice, we can find that freeing balance. This re-mapping requires that we make a practice of exploring, sensing, and tuning in. I will be offering more tools on helping you listen within and connecting to an inner space beyond old patterns and beliefs. You will go where you can set sail courageously into the sea of life, uncertainty, creativity and infinite possibility.

The first exercise gives you a personal experience of Brainspotting using the Self-Spotting: Hearing the Body Exercise. It will help you open the door to heal from within and learn to listen to your body. You will then be able to actually lay new neural pathways with an exercise on believing in yourself, with the You are Magnificent Exercise at the end of the chapter. This part of our voyage is all about the tools you need to dive deeper into your thoughts.

Our voyage started with an overview and headed into the waters of connection. We sailed into the brain and body connection and opened up the possibility of listening within. Let's see how some Self-Spotting can help us get into our own wisdom.

EXERCISES

Self-Spotting: Hearing the Body

This can benefit you to shift from automatic pilot to awareness. It also can help when wanting to release pain in your body.

1. Take a moment to scan your body from the top of your head to the tips of your toes.

2. Find a spot in your body where you feel calm, grounded, and/or connected to your environment and/or inner self. See what that feels like. Spend some time feeling it, notice what it feels like in your muscles, on your skin, and what the smells are around you as you focus on it. Breathe into it. Feel it.

3. Now, gently open your eyes and look around to find someplace that your eyes can relax as you keep feeling this calm, grounded, connected experience.

4. Keeping focusing and noticing.

5. Shift your body to expand into the feeling of being grounded and connected. You may want to tap your hands or feet or stretch a little or maybe rub your hands on the surface you are sitting on to really feel what it is you are connected with.

6. Relax and get into a position that will ensure your comfort and help you feel more relaxed. Get comfortable.

7. Sense/think/say to yourself: *I am here, I am present.*

8. Now, gently let your mind drift to a spot in your body that feels some tension/distress. Focus your attention there, without judgment or expectations. Notice this spot in your body as if you are saying: *Hello, I hear you. I see you.*

9. Try getting to know this spot. Does it have a color, a sound, a tone, a texture? If you could sense it like a part of you, speak to it: *Hello, _____. What is it you want to show me?* Keep your eyes on that calm, grounded spot you found in Step 2, as you connect with curiosity.

10. Let your mind wander and go wherever it needs to go. Now and then, check in with your calm, grounded spot and the part of you that had the tension. Keep doing this for a while.

11. Focus on your breath. Is it shallow or deep? Feel what it is like to breathe in through your nose, then out through your mouth—with your exhale lasting a little longer than your inhale. If you are breathing comfortably through

your nose, that is great. Keep going. Stay curious without forcing anything.

12. Remain curious—questioning and discovering whatever is happening and coming up.

13. Stay with it for as long as you like.

14. When you are ready to end, scan your body again and notice if there is a difference between the tension you started with and now. Is there a difference in how you feel toward the spot that was tense?

15. Take all the time you need, and remember it is something to explore without judgment and expectations.

16. You are in a state of curiosity and wonder—a desire to hear from the stress part like a long-lost friend that has returned home.

17. Maybe ask this body part of yours to write or draw for you. Get to know it and what it may want to tell you. Be creative as you discover something new—or not. Remember, there are no expectations. Whatever comes up is exactly what comes up.

CONNECTING WITH VIBRATION: EXPLORING YOUR CURRENTS

As a reminder, we are all made of electrical currents. Let's work with this electricity and see how we can connect to ourselves as a reliable resource. Later we will be able to achieve even deeper dives into our subconscious and subcortical parts.

This helps to get settled into your energy and charge up if you are feeling a low vibration or to release if you are feeling too much vibration.

1. While doing this, put one hand on your stomach and one on your heart. Wiggle your toes a little. Settle into a seated or standing position.

2. Take a moment to take a few deep breaths—in through your nose and out through your mouth. As you breathe in, fill up your stomach, then your chest, and as you breathe out, empty your chest then your stomach.

3. Keep breathing in and out, noticing your hands moving up and down on your stomach and chest. Feel the air enter your nose and leave your mouth.

4. As your chest expands, let your shoulders go back, and as you exhale, let your shoulders move in ever so gently. This will build up a charge in your body. So as with an electric current, if we have an excess of charge, we need to discharge. As needed, let yourself loosen up some of the energy by shaking your arms and hands and tapping your feet on the ground.

5. Once you have discharged, you can do it again or just simply sit and breathe softly feeling the sensations in your body.

6. Notice how by using your breath and the air around you, you can shift your vibration.

7. If you want to continue, keep your focus on the vibration and gently close your eyes.

YOU ARE MAGNIFICENT

This exercise is helpful for strengthening the connection to yourself without any negative thoughts or to amplify positive ones. It may be hard to consider yourself as magnificent at first, so try it on. I have a friend who always addresses me, "Hello, beautiful." One day I was looking in the mirror with my usual self-talk and decided maybe I should say what she says to address myself. My way had not been helping me feel better. So, I started saying, "Hello, beautiful," to myself. The person in the mirror liked me better. Over time I realized why not keep doing it that way—because everything is subjective, and how I choose to see myself affects the reality I create. If I want to see myself as magnificent, people will also start to see me that way. So, let's give it a try.

1. Find a comfortable position. Take a few deep breaths.

2. As you breathe in and out, feel your back against the surface you are on. Feel your feet against the surface, and relax into your breath. Feel your level of relaxation grow with each breath.

3. Notice the air coming in and going out of your body, especially at the tip of your nose. Feel your chest and stomach rise and fall.

4. Now focus on your skin. Think of it, touch your hand and notice what it feels like. Is it hot, cold, or simply comfortable? Just notice, without judgment. As you feel and think about your skin, consider the pores of your skin. Your skin is the largest organ of your body. Consider how porous you really are.

5. As you breathe in and out, imagine opening up your awareness to how you are connected to all of this: your skin, the surface, your pores and everything your pores take in from your environment. Now, sense the temperature at the surface of your entire body. The pores

keep opening up and taking in all that is around you. This connects you to the inside and outside of the surface of your skin. This opening and closing to the life within and around supports you in being connected to life, to all possibilities. You are connected. You are present with the fullness of life. You are magnificent, and you are connected.

6. Hear/think the words: *You are magnificent.* Say it out loud: *You are magnificent.* Hear the words, open your mind and consider: *You are magnificent.*

7. Keep breathing in and out. Consider the words: *You are magnificent,* and this time repeat them with *I. I am magnificent.* Say it out loud: *I am magnificent.*

8. Now say: *I am connected, I am with the fullness of life. I am magnificent.*

9. Keep doing this for as long as you like, and when you are ready to end the time, bring your focus back to your skin, sense the temperature, sense the texture.

10. Now notice. Notice your skin touching the cloth or the texture of the surface you are on.

11. Breathe in and out. Say the words: *I am here now. I am connected. I am with the fullness of life. I am magnificent.*

You are magnificent for who you are, for all you have lived through, for your willingness to open up and grow. You are magnificent for all you give, and all you are willing to receive. You are magnificent precisely as all humans are wired to be. Yes, we are wired to survive, but we also have been wired with the capacity to think, feel, breathe and live with the best and highest consciousness we desire. We are wired with the gift to choose and decide. We are wired with a consciousness that is endless. We are wired with a deep knowing beyond our thoughts, our understanding and beyond words. We can stay still, and at the same time, we can travel anywhere.

[2]

BECOMING AN INNER EXPLORER

LET'S CONTINUE OUR JOURNEY by exploring our beliefs, how they are formed, and how they create our life experiences. We will now travel deeper with curiosity and discover how to live and thrive, even beyond 3D. Settle in. Your life is going to have a whole new meaning. Let's feel our magnificence!

One day I was preparing to teach a class about creating your own reality. I was unsure what examples to teach, much less how to explain the concept to the class. Then, right before my eyes, an example appeared. As I was pulling into a parking spot, a car appeared in front of me out of thin air. This was New York City, so finding a spot on the street was like finding a needle in a haystack. He wanted the same spot I was claiming. No sooner had I seen his car, a man jumped out and started banging on my window and cursing at me! I was terrified.

Although fear had the best of me, I still knew I had a choice. I could try to hide from him, believing I was bad, wrong, going to get in trouble, and in danger. Or I could feel I was safe, a good person, calm myself down and continue what I was there to do.

I began by taking a walk, finding dinner and heading to class. Walking helped release the fear from my body. It also gave me time to think about my part in the situation. What was going on inside me to create the experience (or reality) of such a situation? Was it a simple misunderstanding, or was I attracting an attack?

In the 45-minute interval between the incident and class, I began to have some perspective and understanding about the incident and discovered some choices I had available. Situations like this give us a possible moment to get curious beyond our initial reactions. When we calm ourselves, we can ask: What is our part? How are we emotionally involved in a situation that is beyond our conscious creation? There can be a temptation to blame and judge, either ourselves or the other person. However, if we don't shift to blame and judgment of ourselves or the other person, we can learn much from the situation.

Situations like my "parking spot moment" give us opportunity to get curious.

At that time in my life, I had a series of incidents where I was verbally attacked. My attackers seemed almost drawn to me by some invisible force. Of course, there was another pattern happening: Even if most people enjoyed my class, I focused on the one student who didn't. I felt that single person was proof of how bad things went. It was as if I was fishing to find something wrong and bad about myself. I was certainly not believing in my own magnificence.

Over time, I continued to get curious and explore beliefs that were affecting my experiences. A real shift began to happen as my awareness increased and I let go of negative beliefs. Recently, I experienced another parking situation. This one, however, turned out quite differently. I connected with a friend, and we switched cars at a spot where I had parked overnight. As she was parking her car where mine had been, a man approached and informed her that the very spot I had been in overnight was a tow-away zone. He pointed to a tiny sign indicating the space was indeed private parking, and that those who parked there would be towed. But I had not seen it! I realized I was beyond fortunate. Not only was I not towed, I was also graciously informed with inexplicable kindness.

Later that evening, yet another person knocked on my car window, asking me, "Did you know you have a flat tire?" No, I did not know. Again, kindness from a stranger kept me safe and protected—no more attacks.

What I know now is, as we change our beliefs and connect to gratitude, people show up differently. Beliefs are that powerful—and often difficult to discern. It is possible to alter them when you know how to spot the patterns and identify the root cause. The exercises at the end of the chapter will help you spot your patterns.

PAUSE: Our brains innately want to find meaning and explanation for our experiences.

FORMING BELIEFS

When we look closer at how beliefs are formed, we begin to see that we create stories from our experiences. Our brains innately want to find meaning and explanation for our experiences. As children, we think in concrete terms and make up generalizations. If something happens once, our young mind takes a snapshot, and we keep referencing the same picture over and over. We feel that is the way life is.

These early life experiences become generalizations we carry into our adult world. They become part of our belief system and rulebook. We think in absolutes, all or nothing, and black or white. As we learn to differentiate and see possibilities, we are able to recognize nuances in life.

The beliefs from our past become the stories we keep telling ourselves. Realizing our storytelling approach gives us more control over what we think, feel and how we want to relate to our personal history—and show up in our life!

Up to now, we have been the Captains of our Ship of Life. Now we are adding a new role within ourselves, the Author. The Author is the part of us who writes the stories. The more we recognize and understand this part of ourselves, we can see the stories we are telling ourselves. We also begin to discover what stories we want to create and develop. With a little guidance, the Author can shift from fictional, habitual thinking and cultural bias to developing all-new material. Authors can shape things into reality, and so can you. Let's dive deeper into our stories and how we can edit them.

MOVING STUCK BELIEFS

I have explored various thought patterns where I felt stuck—even on writing this book. Over the years, many people around me suggested I write one. But, how could I? I was the first grader who sat in the slow reading group. My English SAT scores were 100 points below my math scores, which, candidly, were also not that great.

I dialogued with myself:

Who do I think I am?

I don't know anything.

It's all been said before.

Does my inner self-talk sound familiar to you? My culture supported me in believing these ideas. I heard them said many times. My life experiences "domesticated" me, as Don Miguel calls submitting to our conditioning in his landmark book, *The Four Agreements*. I took in the conditioning and beliefs and made them my own. The exercises at the end of the chapter can help you uncover some of your self-talk and beliefs so your Author can start editing your rulebook.

Your Rulebook

Like many of you, the beliefs I internalized became so rooted in me that I was convinced they were true. But a belief is just deeply convicted thought based on a feeling or emotion.

Let's say an event occurs. Going back to the snapshot metaphor, the brain, much like a camera, takes a photo image. You now have the image in your memory. You then make up a story about that image based on all your physical sensations at the time. You now have a story that becomes the framework for the meaning of similar scenarios, which you then live by. In other words, your story becomes your very own little rulebook. All words and meaning built into this story you just created are unique to you. The information for the story comes from your personal experience, and you are the Author. The story is tried and true, according to the Author—you.

These stories and beliefs have an enormous impact on our lives and behaviors. For example, over the years, I have worked with many female clients who felt trapped. As children, they received mixed messages between being told how wonderful they were, given lavish gifts and doted on, and then being harshly criticized and belittled. Others had parents who encouraged them to get married and have children, or at the least, find a man who would support them. Some of them witnessed their mothers remain socially quiet in their own marriages while obviously in intense emotional pain. They learned by example that they should endure, no matter the cost. This gave them very powerful stories about what love is and how to show it.

These women wrote for themselves certain conclusions about life, men, women, and how to minimize their feelings. They were often cheated on in their marriages. However, they did not feel they had a voice, much less any right to do anything about it, based on their rulebook.

Instead they tried to love and please more, but their situations worsened. The rulebook told them to keep trying or to figure it out. Some had the rule, "You made your bed; now lie in it."

Some of them were abused physically, and others were abused emotionally. Their rulebook said, "Work it out. You can't make it on your own. It is not that bad. Maybe he will ... "

Whatever their story, the situation was unique to each of them. However, what was hauntingly similar was their blind allegiance to a rulebook they felt they had to live by. They lost themselves along the way.

Of course, rulebooks are universal. I have had male clients who were anxious, and they did not understand why. Going through the rulebook, we found things like: Men don't have feelings. Be strong. Be loyal. Work hard. If I don't give in, I will be like my father.

Something like this may have happened to you or may sound familiar. If so, you may have become lost inside your story. We all have certain beliefs, and we shape our life on those beliefs. Still, if you have also felt an inner sense something was not right or needs to change, you are not alone. Happily, this awareness is a hopeful sign.

Over time, the people I've mentioned began to reclaim their own lives. They rediscovered how they were magnificent, and they chose to decide what to believe about themselves instead of what that old rulebook said. They began writing new life stories—and so can you.

CONTINUING TO FIND YOUR INNER GUIDE: SIFTING THROUGH YOUR RULEBOOK

At what point do we set aside powerful conditioning and influencers like our parents and turn toward our own dreams and confidence in our authentic self? What thoughts, feelings and actions do we need to find to support us taking this rebellious action? Turning away from our old stories about who we are and getting curious about what else is possible opens up our awareness for many options we might have believed were not possible for us. I have helped many people over the years to accomplish exactly this.

When I graduated college, I went to find work in New York City. I spent years working in advertising and public relations before deciding to follow my dream as a social worker. My father made no secret that he thought I would fail, and as a result, he gave me very little emotional support. In the end, he even chose not to attend my graduation.

His words, lack of support and absence hurt. However, unlike my mother's milder criticisms, his words did not get under my skin. I was able to hear his point of view and not make it my own. I did go back to school and follow my dream.

> PAUSE: Write down one conditioned belief/habit you have. How was that belief/habit formed? The belief might be something such as: "I am not good enough" or "I keep trying to help, and it is not appreciated."

One of the first steps for moving beyond our conditioning, stories and beliefs is to become aware of them. Once we are aware of these influences, we can discern our own thoughts, ideas, priorities and values. As we understand the beliefs and habits that influence our choices, we can stop acting on autopilot. This is when our Author can really get in and edit our rulebook with different choices.

Jessica was a musician who wanted to play only one instrument, even though she was good with many. She was brought up with the story that she must make up her mind and stick to one thing.

When we act a certain way, because that is how our family (or society) traditionally does things, we are responding the way we were conditioned and told to be. This is acting on autopilot.

Jessica's conditioning of sticking to one thing led to a great deal of anxiety for her. She was left feeling lost and confused. Jessica described it as being locked up inside—knowing something was wrong, and realizing she needed help. She became familiar with the beliefs which were driving her automatic pilot responses and stunting her creativity. Like Jessica, getting to know our beliefs that we are choosing is key for feeling free and authentic.

One of my favorite client exercises for understanding our negative beliefs and the resulting internal negative talk comes from Dr. Daniel Amen. He has been scanning brains for over 25 years. He found certain parts of the brain get stuck in negative thinking, based on conditioning and habits. His written exercise, designed to eliminate these automatic thoughts, is called ANTs (Automatic Negative Thoughts). He references different roles the ANTs play, such as a Fortune Teller predicting the worst possible outcome. Another ANT presents by beating oneself up with guilt and the "shoulds and supposed to's." Amen states these automatic responses contribute to depression, stroke, anxiety and many other ailments.

Another way to shift from our automatic rulebook responses is to assess our priorities and values. Which ones do you want to live by, and which ones do you want to let go? For example, had I been more grounded in my values I would not have been worried about my mother's opinion regarding the house I was buying. I would have had "thicker skin" with a better boundary between myself and others. Having clear priorities and values leads to clear boundaries and stronger relationships.

> PAUSE: List some things that really matter to you. How are those things related to your priorities and boundaries? Which ones are similar or different to what you were brought up with? At the end of this chapter is an Exercise on Priorities and Values that can help you dive deeper. Finding our core values helps us live authentically.

Jess is an example of someone who was not living by his priorities and values. He had many beliefs that involved fear of rejection, that he didn't matter, and worry about what others thought of him. His strongest fear of all was fear of performing. Each of these fears was the result of his early conditioning. He learned to live according to what pleased people. It was equivalent to survival for him.

Jess discovered that he was so focused on what others thought he did not have a sense of himself at all. In our work, he got curious around how he went about pleasing people. He looked at how he would try to manipulate them into liking him, giving him what he wanted. Eventually, he noticed his intention to get something from others left him feeling disconnected, empty and depressed.

As Jess became more curious and aware of his actions, he acted them out less and less. He realized he was sensitive and caring and naturally liked to give without expectation. He also learned he had wonderful talents to share with the world. His depression lifted as he lived more authentically from his own priorities and values instead of trying to figure out what others wanted and then trying to please them.

OUR MOTHERS' DAUGHTERS AND OUR FATHERS' SONS

As mentioned, our beliefs are adopted from our upbringing and the environment around us. These habits, rituals and routines are taught over time and become automatic responses. Many times, these habits run so deep they appear as part of our personality. We rarely question it, as it feels so natural.

I remember being in Temple with my mother and asking her during a prayer, "Why do you say that?" Her response was an unsatisfying, "Because we do."

I was brought up in a community where children were to be seen and not heard. That interaction set a tone. I learned to keep quiet and answer my own questions in private. Unfortunately, we didn't have Google at the time.

PAUSE: How about you? Did you have an opportunity to question the beliefs and patterns of your upbringing? Do you use expressions such as: "That is how we do it in my family," or "My parents told me" or how about "I just learned to be that way from my father."

We often seem to feel we have no choice. In these moments, we feel we are victims of our circumstances. I have discovered it does not have to be that way. I invite you to explore your choices and beliefs.

We have a strong need to belong, which makes it hard to let go of our conditioning. A key way to belong is to please those to whom we want to be connected. It is a reward system, where we receive praise and acceptance for pleasing. We follow the rules, the life patterns and style of those who raise us, and then we get rewarded with love. As adults, we experience this in our jobs. You follow the company rules and gain benefits and promotions. Or sometimes, you follow a person's request even if it is not mandated, but the desire to connect is so intense you will go against your values to try and please. You will get a better understanding of your values in the Priorities and Values Exercise at the end of this chapter.

PAUSE: What rules have you been following? What people have you tried to please—even if you did not feel great about what you did?

I notice this intense desire to please, especially in conflict with our personal value, often occurs in love relationships. One partner wants the other to do something the other does not feel right about. The second partner will do it anyway because they want to please and be connected. The one who goes along usually doesn't say anything about their discomfort, but over time, they get resentful, needy, or act out in another disconnecting behavior. Paradoxically, they often end up getting what was feared most—rejection and disconnection.

Has that ever happened to you in any relationship? Think about yourself in relationships and how you may have done something to please someone else, even if it was not what you wanted. Or another situation where you ended up getting the exact thing you feared the most—being left alone, rejected, resented, disrespected, etc.

When we discover our values and uncover some beliefs that might not serve us, we are ready to look at how we may have abandoned personal values to get love. It happens more often than you might imagine, and it isn't always easy to admit. Once we discover we abandoned our values for love and we want to choose differently, we have more freedom and no longer feel like victims of our circumstances.

I have worked with many women who loved men who didn't give them the attention they craved. When the woman paid more attention to him, hoping for a loving connection, the man would get annoyed. This pattern would escalate, as she tried to please him to greater degrees, being continuously disappointed, until, finally, he leaves. Then to add insult to injury, he finds a strong woman who stands up to him. The book *Why Men Love Bitches* by Sherry Argov explores this phenomenon quite effectively.

Of course, the converse is also true. Many of my male clients have tried to please a woman and feel like no matter how hard they try, their attempts are never enough. Often these men go along, doing what the woman wants, but sooner or later, he blows up when she requests one thing too many. This results in a fight, and he feels blamed because he got angry. But behind that anger, what made him try so hard to please? Whatever your gender, we are all seeking connection.

Sooner or later, we discover the desire to please at the expense of our own value system and magnificence is not worth it. Choosing to live from our values provides us with the freedom to show up authentically.

On a physical level, when we choose differently, the brain literally shifts neural pathways and synapse connections. This is because as we learn new things, our brain engages in synaptic pruning, deleting the neural connections that are no longer needed, while strengthening the necessary connections. It is much like reprogramming a computer. Instead of disposing of the computer, we can just change the program.

Mavin, who was highly conflicted, is a beautiful example. She wanted to do something with a friend and was afraid it would upset her relationship with another friend. Speaking up was a major challenge in her life. We focused on the inner critic that told her what she wanted was "bad" and "stupid." We had her imagine this inner critic as a cartoon character. During the session, she began to see the cartoon character was much like her parents. It spoke to her critically, much as they had. As the session continued, Mavin noticed she felt exactly as she did as a child.

We often treat ourselves the way we have been treated. Mavin realized she had internalized and perpetuated this criticism of herself. She worried if she gave up the self-criticism that she would somehow be disrespecting her parents. People often resist giving up parts of their rulebook because they don't want to disrespect their loved ones.

I gave the following explanation, which she found very helpful: Growing up is much like having our hand in some dirt. When we take our hands out of the dirt, some is left on our hands. That residue dirt does not come off so easily. Clearing some of our beliefs and pains from the past is like clearing the dirt off our hands. Choosing to let go of certain habits and harmful ways of treating ourselves is not necessarily disrespectful. Those behaviors may not be ours to begin with.

There's no judgment needed of what is right or wrong. Treating yourself with kindness may be your approach. Your parents' way of relating may be just a different approach. You can wash your hands of it without disrespecting them.

Several examples of beliefs I have seen that can be washed off include:

- I don't know who I am.
- I am not good enough.
- I will never meet anyone.
- I don't know how to be a friend.
- Something bad always happens to me.
- I can't do this.

Beliefs that sound final are often good ones to wash off. The Washing Your Hands Exercise at the end of this chapter will help you find a way to discover what to keep and what to let go.

YOU BE YOU

Often people say they feel anxious and think it is all physical. They aren't entirely wrong. Anxiety is definitely physical, but like every sensation, it has a root cause. Did you behave and think a certain way that caused the anxiety? When we live according to other people's values or please someone to avoid rejection, we live with fear—and it shows up in our bodies as anxiety.

Remember, we are social beings, and we thrive and grow in connection with others. As the saying goes, "No man is an island unto himself," so it is natural to want to be connected. However, when we view our connection as adversarial, thinking it is either us or them, we create a damaging disconnection from self.

I often hear people say, "I was feeling great about myself, but once I began a relationship with _____, I lost myself. I exercise much less. I am not eating as well. I stopped doing the things I loved."

We lose ourselves when we feel we can be present for the other or for ourself, but not both.

When we feel our choices are limited, we tend to think in absolutes such as: *It is either all or nothing. It is either them or me.* This is dualistic thinking, which is fear-based. Fear can show up in our bodies as pain and illness; our feelings as loneliness, sadness, anger or negative thoughts. It also shows up as anxiety.

The invitation here is to get curious about your pains and discover the lessons they have to offer.

Surrender to the voyage.

When we open up and consider there is something to gain from a painful experience, we decide to surrender to something greater. We drop our protective posture.

I invite you to surrender to the voyage. I am offering you that opportunity right here. Learn what your automatic responses are, rewrite the outdated rulebook you have lived by, and discover your connection to more possibilities for yourself. As we tap into the electric current of life, we have greater access to the expanded consciousness that is always available to us.

How Things Are Supposed To Be

I had a long, often disappointing, journey of trying to have a child. Eventually, I had to let go of the rulebook on how families are formed. When I was around others who were starting families, or when I was asked when I would join the ranks of parents, I covered up my pain and shame with, "I'm not ready yet."

I was comparing my situation to others and naming it as bad and wrong. I felt something was wrong with me. That was my belief. It was a self-created one because my life was not lining up with my rulebook. I was acting from that belief and got stuck until I could embrace my true desire of being a mother and let go of others' judgments—or judgments I thought they had—about my life.

In truth, my family did not require that I have a child. They also had no agenda of how that had to happen. I was lost down a rabbit hole of disappointment that was entirely of my own making.

We can all get lost in the Wonderland of our own rulebook, thinking things are supposed to be a certain way. This blocks the real power of our imagination to create the outcome we desire. Our fear, anticipation of worst-case scenarios, and worry keep us stuck. We can feel so small and unworthy when we worry about what others think and compare ourselves to them. Not only that, fighting for what we think is right disconnects us from our reality.

Life has its ups and downs, and how we choose to think can create a better reality. A shift in our thinking produces an outcome that inevitably has a timing of its own. So, be patient and keep working on your rulebook. Edit your rulebook as you go along, and expect to see results for your effort.

DIVING DEEP

Getting curious about our pain is much like the infinity symbol. We go up one side as we gain strength and awareness, then we dive down into our unconscious material that rises up to meet our awareness, gets integrated, and then we dive down again. Each time around the loop, time spent going down into our unconscious becomes shorter, and our strengths expand. We have already built up some strength for ourselves in Chapter 1 when we connected to our magnificence.

Before we leave looking at beliefs, let's look at culture, faith and religion.

CULTURE, FAITH, RELIGION

People of various faiths occasionally enter therapy for spiritual healing. Some were traumatized by other people's actions in their shared religious teaching or in their spiritual home. This is a very core trauma that impacts many basic attachments: to God, spiritual force, and other humans. If we add to that the essential need for connection and belonging, we are terrified to explore our beliefs, lest they prove inadequate, or even speak up out of disloyalty. You may have similar experiences.

Ultimately, there is a big difference between religious or spiritual teachings and the people who teach them. Many of my clients have become very lost, confused, angry, and distrustful because of the way they were taught about religion or spirituality. It is an important distinction that how they were taught is not necessarily a reflection on the teachings themselves. Still, each of us may feel these wounds differently, based on our experiences.

One time, I was part of a spiritual non-denominational community, and several people were joining a pyramid scheme. They told me they had "guidance" that it was okay. I felt in my gut something was off. Peer pressure and the desire to belong had me feeling confused and conflicted. I had to consider whether I should listen to my instinct or follow the group.

Religious groups often have so much influence that we get lost. The social connection in us is so strong we may think this is our way without question, as mentioned earlier with Lieberman's work.

We each experience our intuition differently, from seeing signs and symbols imbued with meaning, to visions, dreams, synchronicities, or just a good old "gut feeling." Whatever it is for you, begin to look for and notice the difference between the rulebook and your inner truth. In Chapter 5, we will expand on developing our intuition.

THE SECRET OF EXPLORING

You might find it difficult to follow your inner truth or deeply explore your conditioned beliefs. The reason for this difficulty is usually that the questions touch on taboo topics that have not risen before to your consciousness. Examples of this could be a counter-cultural desire to marry outside of your faith, or someone of the same sex or a different race, switch careers or move out of the country. There is nothing wrong with any of these choices. Still, you may feel disloyal to a person or group of people if you consider being or acting differently. It is as if you lived in a time when everyone thought the world was flat, and you would be ridiculed if you thought it might be round.

STICK WITH IT AND PAUSE

Be curious about the traditions, patterns and customs you grew up with. It is possible you may have written your story so well, you did not know there were other ways to live. Instead of thinking of it as a challenge, I suggest thinking of it as an adventure into the unknown. Let yourself become fearless. Keep sailing—you won't fall off.

When I started looking at the beliefs I grew up with, I blamed myself for everything that had gone wrong because I was living with the idea that I am responsible for my own reality. Whether that is true or not, I approached myself with a very harsh attitude. My self-esteem suffered. My experience is common, because we often treat ourselves the way we were treated. We judge and criticize ourselves the way we felt judged and criticized. It is a bit paradoxical that we treat ourselves how the culture we grew up in treated us, and that is the very thing we are questioning.

> PAUSE: How can we change our approach if we have no other models to go by?

We need support, and we need some resources to help us get started. As we continue, use the exercises at the end of each chapter to take a deeper dive and to keep uncovering how you are your own role model. We will look at how to create and develop what we desire in Chapter 3. Once you realize you are innately magnificent, you are well on your way to realizing your authentic self.

PAUSE: *Journal, dance, if you want to, take a walk, and consider your experience.*

EXERCISES:

FINDING BELIEFS

This exercise will help you find some core beliefs.

1. For the next week, write a description of your day from waking up to sleeping. Note any problems, frustrations or challenging connections with people. Just a very short description is needed as we are looking for common themes/patterns to get to core beliefs that drive you. Example: *Woke tired today, did my meditation and exercised, felt happier, went to work and got into traffic. I hate traffic, can't stand having to sit still. Turned on some music, good sounds and got to office/school eager to start the new project/meet friends/ learn from____. Things moved fast and felt relatively okay. Not too bad. Came home and crashed.* Next day: *Woke, had strange dream, can't remember, no classes, watched TV, got bored, shot some hoops, felt better, hung with friends, not very eventful ...* Continue for a week.

2. Notice any themes that repeat from day to day. Even if you did not jot it down this week, something may come to mind as you are noticing and looking for patterns. As you review, look for phrases you use, moods, emotions,

and/or encounters with people. In the example above, the theme may be about uneventful days.

3. Inquire on the theme. How often does this happen over the past several months/years? Where else have I noticed this theme/pattern? Has this been a family trait, a learned pattern from friends or relatives, a state of mind I have fallen into?

4. How does this serve me? I don't mean positively per se. Often when we continue to do things unconsciously, we may be gaining something from it, and at the same time, there is a price we are paying. For example, *as long as things are uneventful, I don't have to risk making mistakes.* We can then see that risking making mistakes is a fear-based thought. *The price I pay for this is not having more adventures in my life and going after jobs or subjects of interest to me.*

5. When I follow these thoughts and these patterns: I feel sad/bored/happy/glad/apathetic/purposeless. All our attitudes will lead to feelings and actions. What feelings and actions does this belief bring to you? Reflect on these feelings and see if you can explore the feeling a little with a meditation.

6. Having sat with the feelings, what conclusions or new thinking have you discovered?

7. Having choice: Once you sat with and explored the feelings and the belief, is there anything about this belief /attitude you would like to be different?

PRIORITIES AND VALUES

Priorities and values are central to our sense of self and our self-esteem. This exercise is helpful for clarity on what matters most to us and how we want to be in life from our authentic self.

Start with some reflection.

1. What were your parents/primary caregivers' values around money? School? Work?
2. What were their values around religion? Tradition? Getting together with family and/or friends?
3. What were their thoughts and values around status?
4. From the above list, write which values you continue to follow in your life now.
5. What were the values you grew up with around exercise? Was exercise competitive or for fun? Did you play competitive sports? What values did your family have around that?
6. What values did you learn regarding health? How often did you see doctors? Did you go to school when sick? Did your parents work when sick? How often did you have dental checkups? What type of food did you eat growing up? Did you have seated meals? Fast food dinners? Who cooked and prepared meals?
7. From these experiences, what values do you continue to put toward exercise and health?

Now that you have reflected on the values you grew up with, let's look further into things that impact you.

1. What are three things that make you happy? Sad? Laugh?

2. Who do you admire and what traits do you admire the most?

3. Do you mimic anyone? If so, who and why?

4. How do people describe you?

5. Do you have a favorite book, movie, story? If so, what is the main message that impacts you the most?

6. What are three things that you must experience with another in a relationship? For example, they have to be honest, playful, and can get serious when needed.

7. Do you have any key things that bother you the most that you would never want to do?

After all the reflecting from above, write some key words which define your core values. Example words may include: health, generosity, responsibility, integrity, respect, authenticity, kindness.

BACK TO SELF

One client reported using this exercise with noticeable improvement whenever he felt ungrounded. See what happens for you.

1. Bring your hands together. Together they represent all of you.

2. Now, have your right hand represent the part of you seeking approval, love and acceptance from others. Move your right hand slowly away from your left hand. As you do this, notice the space between your hands. The left hand is hanging there, representing the part of you that senses something is missing.

3. Now, continue to notice the space between your right hand and your left hand.

4. Consider how it feels to have gone that far away from yourself.

5. Now, slowly see what happens when you move your hands together. Be certain to move slowly.

6. How does it feel to come back to yourself?

7. Journal on your experience.

WASHING YOUR HANDS

1. Write a list of three things you hear yourself say that sound like you learned them from your family/culture. Example:

   a. *Children should be seen and not heard.*

   b. *You made your bed, now you better lie in it.*

   c. *Two wrongs don't make a right.*

2. When did you start hearing this? *These are things I remembered from the time I was very little.*

3. How do you feel when you hear it? *Punished.*

4. Do you live by these statements? *Yes. They come to me without thinking.*

5. Let's now start to wash some of these statements away one at a time.

   a. Choose one situation to start with.

   b. Breathe in and out. Imagine yourself going from your place to a wooded or sandy area. As you start to walk there in your mind's eye, see what it feels like to move from your left foot to your right foot. As you move from side to side, you are going closer to a beautiful area filled with nature sounds. Notice the sounds. Smell the air. Look around. Feel the air touching your skin. Notice something catching your eye. It is a beautiful body of water. You can't help but settle in and stare at it. As you look into the water you relax and feel more and more comfortable. Your mind and body relax. You begin to contemplate the statement you started with. You connect to moments in time when you or another person used this statement. You feel various sensations. As you continue to be with what comes up, at a certain point you decide to rest your hands in the water and let the water wash away what is no longer yours to live by. You start to think of new ways to understand and approach situations where you previously acted on automatic pilot. You feel soothed and refreshed. When you are ready, you slowly leave and return to the location you started. At your own speed, slowly open your eyes. Move around and stretch to return to feeling calm, grounded and connected.

c. Journal about your insights.

BALL OF LIGHT: CLEANSING OUR ENERGY

We will now do a visualization of cleansing your energy I call the Ball of Light.

This will help you clear your body's energy for more vitality. We will start with imagining a ball of light at the top of your head and have the ball slowly roll down and clear out your energy.

1. Find a comfortable position. Sitting is ideal for this exercise.

2. Sense a ball of light at the top of your head. This ball of light will slowly grow as it descends and gathers all the negative thoughts, feelings, and sensations that are weighing you down.

3. Imagine the ball of light having a violet light. Notice how bright the violet light is. Have it start to gather particles of busy thoughts, blocked ideas, fears, and worries blocking you from being open-minded and feeling peace around connection. Let all that is not supporting your guidance, wisdom, and inner strength gather onto the ball.

4. Now notice it coming into your forehead in the area between your eyes. Many people call this area the third eye. Notice an indigo light. Let all that is blocking your vision and willingness to see the beauty of life gather on the ball of light. Let all that is blocking you from seeing with greater consciousness and clarity gather on the ball.

5. Now watch it continue to roll into your throat area turning into a blue light. Here all those things that are blocking you from self-expression, speaking your truth, needs, inner voice, and creativity gather onto the ball.

6. The ball continues to roll toward your heart and chest with a green glow to it. Let all that is affecting your heart area gather onto the ball, such as loneliness, resentment, grief or loss.

7. It continues to roll down into your upper stomach area with a yellow light. Let all that is not supporting your wisdom and intuition gather onto the ball, such as self-doubt, the opinions of others, and ideas of unworthiness.

8. The ball continues to roll into your lower stomach with the color orange. Let all that is negatively impacting your relationships go onto the ball. Watch your thoughts continue to move onto the ball.

9. The ball continues to roll to the base of your spine and takes on the color red. Let all that impacts your self-worth gather onto the ball.

10. See the ball continuing to move down your body out your lower spine and lower legs all the way through the floorboards of the building you are in.

11. Let it roll through the foundation, into the soil and all the layers of the earth, into the waters, all the way to the molten lava. May the fire transform it into clarity and beauty.

[3]

REDIRECTING THOUGHTS

NOW WE ARE REALLY SAILING! On our voyage, we have discovered connection to the air, the breath, people, our bodies, our cells, our culture and our families. We looked at our rulebook, which includes our beliefs, priorities and values. This chapter is about editing that rulebook.

CHANGING YOUR MIND

Once you are aware of how your past patterns make you feel and act, you can choose to notice your responses and think through your actions. Some people can make changes simply by talking through and thinking about things. It is all they need to reframe their thoughts and change their behavior. For others, all the talk in the world will not shift deep unconscious patterns. They need to work with their body to unlock stuck thoughts. For everyone, working with the body can actually change the mind.

I have been successfully helping clients using a powerful, focused treatment method called Brainspotting. Brainspotting taps into a person's innate wisdom to heal body and mind. It has helped clients shift past deeply ingrained, limiting beliefs such as: something is wrong with me, it's all my fault, and I keep trying, but nothing works.

As mentioned previously, Brainspotting uses the brain/body relationship and focused mindfulness. Our senses collect information from our environment. Our brain interprets the information collected by our body in this way. Brainspotting provides a supportive framework to sort through what information we want to keep and what we want to let go. Simply put, it is based on "where you look affects how you feel." If you are thinking of something, such as something is wrong with me, and feeling a tightness in your stomach, if you look to the right, you may feel different than when you look straight or to the left.

A typical Brainspotting session usually involves the client having an issue to work on, feeling a body sensation when thinking of that issue, and then finding an eye position that relates to the body sensations when thinking of the issue. Once finding the eye position, the client keeps their eyes fixed in focused mindfulness. Various internal sensations, images, dialogue or other internal experiences come up inside the client. The client can talk as much or as little as desired during a session, which is very helpful as the brain and body often shift from thought to thought. Body pains, wiggles, twitches or other sensations may be experienced.

If you aren't working with a therapist, sitting with an understanding friend can be very healing. The Self-Spotting

Exercise at the end of Chapter 1 is a tool to shift your brain and body to help edit your rulebook.

Many present-day reactions and relationship patterns that we get caught in are based on past experiences. Brainspotting is extremely helpful to differentiate the past from the present and feel free from behavioral patterns that keep us stuck.

For example, once Claire was in a session, feeling distraught, abandoned and upset because her boyfriend at the time did not respond to her text. The more she stayed focused on her eye spot and was in a deep focused mindfulness, she started to recall memories of when her father left the family when she was three and how her mother was never around to help her. As the older memories surfaced, she was able to feel compassion for her younger self. Over many months she was able to become kinder to herself, and although she continued to be annoyed by her boyfriend from time to time, she did not feel it as a personal attack in the same way.

We can learn to change course and rewrite our rulebook. A process we discussed earlier, called neuroplasticity, is a way our brains can change and grow. Our brains are able to form and reorganize connections, especially in response to learning, experience or as the result of an injury. This can have long-lasting, life-changing results. I see it happen every day in my practice.

Remember the important idea we discussed in Chapter 1, where Donald Hebb, states, "Neurons that fire together, wire together." This means as we change our thoughts, we rewire our brain, and thus, our rulebook gets edited.

You Can Direct Your Experience

As we shift and rewire, we start to experience life differently. Instead of being lost in patterns, we become far more creative, and life experiences start to flow more easily. We began our voyage as Captains of the ship. We met the Author of the rulebook. We met the Editor. Now let's meet the Artist.

The Artist will help us create experiences. Our Artist's palette contains four key ingredients. If the picture is not coming out the way the Artist wants, the Artist can blend the paint colors further for richer, deeper hues. Let's see how.

The Four Colors

1. Desire
2. Intention/Decision
3. Imagination
4. Expectation

To start, we need desire. Desire is the fiery red color. It shows up as a passion or a longing, and we will feel it in our bodies. It will have a certain emotion, charge, and intensity. Next, we establish an intention to move toward the desire. Intention is your brilliant yellows that pop off the canvas. Intention's intensity is amplified by an image (imagination) we hold of what the desire fulfilled will feel like—a vivid green of growth and abundance. Lastly, a certain degree of expectation holds the rest of the hues in place, with its clear, brilliant blue.

Saying Yes: Aligning With Desire

Saying "Yes" to your intention opens you up to various possibilities and surprises. Listen to your environment with openness and wonder. You do not have to figure out all the details. Be willing; get out of the way. Trust the unexpected. When we set intention, we leave room for uncertainty. Success demands we keep an open mind for the unexpected. We are now aligning our conscious thoughts with our desire. Maybe you already set your desire but have not consciously thought about it in a long time.

When we were little, we may have fantasized about growing up with such phrases as: *When I grow up, I want to...* In an early edition of the book, *What Color is Your Parachute*, Richard Bolles suggested you think about what games you liked to play when you were younger. For example, I used to love playing school. I may have planted a thought deep in my subconscious. Along the way, in my career I watched therapists who were teachers. Deep inside I set an intention.

PAUSE: What did you wish to be or do when you were growing up? Is it connected to your desire now?

With a blank canvas we can create whatever picture we want. We are painting now beyond our rulebook. Let's keep painting.

INTENTION AND DECISION

If I desire something, splashing vibrant red everywhere, but go no further, I must pause and get curious: *Do I really want it? Do I think I am supposed to have it? Is there something else I need first? What is it I really desire?* Many desires are simply a passing fancy and do not take hold.

As you become curious, you may realize you thought you were saying "yes" to a desire when you are really saying "no." Or, the little voice inside may be saying, *Yes but...* which inevitably means your desire won't get met.

For example, George was depressed and knew exercising would shift his mood, yet he had little motivation. In session he was working on the part of him that said "no" and started to ask, "Now what am I supposed to do?" Instead of giving him an instruction, he got curious about the phrase "What am I supposed to do?"

He began to realize his lack of motivation was a reaction to a rulebook expectation he had of himself. He started to make connections to past experiences, his body released tension and at the end of the session he was ready to set a true intention—the vibrant yellow—in a way that felt right to him.

Jessica, the musician, wanted to unleash her creativity in ways she had felt confined before. She worked during our sessions as well as in between sessions, noticing how her brain and body reacted when she was feeling anxious. She began to re-label her anxiousness as "worry thoughts" which allowed her to observe them neutrally rather than believing them. She also started doing more exercise and meditation.

Months after our therapy ended, she wrote a great thank you letter telling that all the things she was hoping to work toward had manifested. For example, she had a desire to go back to school but was missing deadlines and not putting together her application. Jessica realized she was not sticking to her intention, and that directly affected the outcome of her desire. As she gained more awareness and aligned with her intention, things started to flow. She had more energy and more passion. She started to speak to people about her vision and received support and connections. She was a great example of having the decision and intention to stick to the practices she needed for change to happen.

Having a gauge to assess how strongly you are willing and ready to work toward an intention is a good approach. The number 80 percent is often used to gauge readiness. When you are planning to set your intention on a desire, ask yourself, "Am I ready and willing to work toward this at least 80 percent, or is there something else I need to shift first?"

You Always Have a Choice

Too many people have survived horrible traumas, whether caused by a parent, priest, friend, relative, car or world disaster. These traumas inevitably impact their attitudes; however, healing is possible, even in the most severe cases. With healing, they, like all of us, are able to reorganize their thoughts and choose a new way to see themselves in the world. They can course correct and start to choose new thoughts as we discussed before regarding neuroplasticity. They can start to say "yes" to their new thoughts and new direction.

We may not always be able to decide what to do or what is true, but we can decide to reframe our perspective. Right now, as I am writing this book, a bird flew into my house. Is the bird free or captured? Are we free or captured by our thoughts? The more we make questions like these our habit, the easier it is to recognize various perspectives.

Viktor Frankl speaks to this in his book *In Search of Meaning*. He demonstrated that Holocaust victims' approach to their reality had a strong impact on how they dealt with such horrific circumstances. He addressed the fact that as humans we have the liberty to be spiritually free in any situation. His insights recognized that even in the face of death and the worst circumstances no one can take away our freedom to choose our attitudes. In his words, "to choose one's own way."[8]

IMAGINATION

The vivid green of imagination is the color of creativity. There are really no limits on our imagination—except the ones we choose to impose on ourselves based on what we believe is possible.

Harry was ready to move out of state, open a shop and start a family. We did a creative visualization exercise. If you want to try something similar go to the Visualization Into a New State Exercise at the end of this chapter. For Harry, it was to feel free from a corporate setting, have more independence, be in an intimate relationship and start a family. He worked on the underlying beliefs around having to be in Corporate America in order to make enough money to support a family. He felt stifled by society's norms. Over the year we worked together, he overcame childhood negative experiences and became more self-confident, met new friends and decided to move out west. After our work ended, he wrote a lovely note describing his life and how everything from the visualization came true.

Creative visualization is a mindfulness practice. The work used with Harry came from those taught by Shakti Gawain in *Creative Visualization: Use the Power of Your Imagination to Create What You Want in Your Life.*

Some key components include connecting to your desire with all your senses, having a body felt sense of the experience you are desiring, envisioning it and sensing it as if it is happening in present time. Once you have the clear picture, and really feel it as if it is your present reality, state: May this, or something greater, come to me easily and effortlessly.

You may also want to write it out, do a vision board or paint a picture to expand on the felt sense of this possibility.

PAUSE: *May this, or something greater, come to me easily and effortlessly.*

Imagination can be extremely powerful when we align our energy with it. Brain studies show mental imagery impacts the cognitive processes in the brain, supports motor control, attention and planning. It has also been found that imagination-focused practices increase self-confidence and improve performance in all activities—not just sports.

If you are stuck imagining a picture of your desire, begin to think about what it feels like to have this desire fulfilled. Sense how it may sound or smell. What will you say, do or wear? What will your surroundings look like? Who will you be around? The more we can add our different senses into our imagination the stronger it becomes. We are taking different parts of our physical energy into a whole new space. It is like preparing a movie set and then putting yourself in the movie.

I recently asked a client who was feeling stuck if she could imagine herself being different. She said "no." Some of her "no" was because no one around her was mirroring enough positivity for her to develop a good sense of self. We began to work on her imagining herself differently. As her imagination was activated, she started recognizing and receiving positive comments from others which then shifted her internal sense of self.

I share a couple of ways to receive positive comments yourself in the Receiving Positive Comments Exercise at the end of this chapter.

EXPECTATIONS

Lastly, a certain degree of expectation holds the rest of the hues in place, with its clear, brilliant blue. Al-Anon, a 12-Step Recovery Program, teaches that our expectations are pre-meditated disappointments waiting to happen. Creative visualization teaches us to expect what we desire. Could both be true? Don't expect something and at the same time expect it?

Yes. Both our definition and frame of reference regarding the expectation impact the outcome. If I desire something and expect it, but it doesn't happen, there are many possible reasons. It may be out of my control entirely. Or it may not have been a realistic expectation. More subtle reasons include that my desire was not clear, or I did not really believe I could have what I expected and thought it was just wishful thinking. The subtle reasons of clarity or disbelief require a clearing of our unconscious and letting go of any hidden rigidity.

For myself, I desired to have a family for years. I expected that meant I get pregnant, have a baby, and thus, a family. However, it turns out my design of a family was different than how I thought it would occur. I remained clear about the desire itself, and as I worked with various options—including fertility treatments that were also disappointing—I ultimately found adoption provided the fulfillment of my desire for family. All to say, I held the expectation softly, staying with the desired outcome, not the specific path to get there.

One day I was sitting in my office realizing everyone I had seen that day shared something in common. Each person in one form or another was in pain because someone in their life was not doing things the way they wanted. This is a self-induced pain to shift.

Three main mindsets which sabotage our desires and create unmet expectations are: Pride, Self-will and Fear. They are separate, yet they work together in our beliefs especially when it comes to desiring something.

If I desire something, but my unconscious thoughts are:

If I don't get this, I am a failure.

I know I am better than ... therefore I deserve ...

or other thoughts around being better or worse than another person, then my mind is closed to possibility.

Our expectations get stuck when fear and a sense of forcing something to happen are present. They also get stuck when we expect something to happen at the expense of another. If I am pushing something to be a certain way then I think I know best—but then I am scared I won't get my way and am also scared I will be wrong. And, I may be pushing because I deserve it more than anyone else. This is how pride, self-will and fear work together and keep us stuck. We become stuck in our belief, pushing to get what we want, proving our belief is correct, scared we will get rejected and be wrong.

Forcing things can show up as frustration, withdrawal, wishing and hoping something or someone will change, but doing nothing to assert ourselves. Additionally, "forcing" can appear as behaviors that are controlling, combative, or demanding. Fear shows up as the idea that everything may not work out, creating tremendous anxiety.

When we are filled with pride, self-will and fear we are unlikely to remain open to unexpected opportunities and creative solutions, which often are far better results than what we were expecting. We overlook them, and they pass us by—when they had been right within our grasp had we been in the right mindset.

I was working with a young man around his pattern of getting angry and breaking up relationship after relationship. He desired a loving relationship, but his pride, self-will and fear kept getting in the way. He would often feel competitive with his partner. Competition is about pride and fear. This made him angry, and he used his self-will to try and get her to agree to certain things in the relationship. They would fight, and eventually she broke up. When we looked at his relationship patterns, he was able to see where he participated in the problem with his outbursts and accusations. He also got to connect to when this first started in his life. Opening up the connection helped him heal his younger self from feeling neglected and less than others. Getting curious helped him rework his canvas and move toward the lifestyle he longed for.

An example of how life can show up really different than we planned is when I was 26, on a quest to become a mother, I went to the first doctor who said that if I was 19 and unwed this would be easy. Now, did I plant a negative belief in my subconscious, or was there another plan for how I was to have a family already set in motion? This is where the need to have an open mind and soften around our expectations is important.

After that appointment I did not become pregnant and I went on a 12-year journey of working with doctors, prayer, meditation and seeing healers. During those 12 years I learned about creative visualization and manifestation. Personally, I found it frustrating. I was doing what I was being taught, and nothing (by my expectations) was happening. Or was it? I was certainly not the only person involved in the desire. There were two other people to help my desire manifest—the father and the child.

The horoscope woman told me I would be pregnant by February—which didn't happen. My lesson was to surrender and not be attached to the outcome.

Looking back is much easier than being there at the time. In retrospect I can say I had the exact child my family needed—the father, my child and myself. Yet, it happened so differently than what I expected! In retrospect I realize in my imagination I saw myself with a child, but I don't recall seeing myself pregnant. I was focusing on having a child. And I did; we adopted a beautiful child. I am grateful for her and the life we all have. We had many lessons along the way. Working with imagination is very specific, so keep working with your canvas and adjust the image as you see fit.

RADICAL FORGIVENESS: A WIDE LENS OF UNDERSTANDING

Another lesson I learned along the way which can help with releasing expectations and helps us redirect our thoughts is radical forgiveness. Radical forgiveness refers to looking at the bigger picture of something. It can be very helpful when we feel hurt or upset. When I can see things from a wider lens, I can let go of my way of how things have to be. I can start to understand how different people and different timing and experiences fit into whatever it is I thought I desired.

Colin Tipping refers to this in his teachings on Radical Forgiveness, when he speaks about accepting what has happened, and learning what the situation has to offer. I often call these experiences "my Buddhas." Each experience—especially a challenging one—is an opportunity to grow beyond what I feel about it. Seeing a larger picture helps open up to new learning and opens our mind to the unexpected. Colin Tipping's Four-Step Process can be found at: https://www.radicalforgiveness.com/ pdf/Four%20Steps%20To%20Radical%20Forgiveness.pdf

Forgiveness can be complex and difficult when we have been wounded by trauma and/or betrayal. This is also true where there is deep sadness, grief and pain from another's actions. It can take time and deep work to consider letting go of resentment, anger, frustration and the attachment to punishing the perpetrator. Throughout the process, remember that forgiveness does not make the perpetrator's actions right. Forgiveness is a letting go of any wish or expectation someone else will change. There is tremendous peace and freedom when we stop holding on. To continue doing so causes you pain and stops you from experiencing what you desire.

In Chapter 1 we spoke of energy and how we are made of electric currents. That means all our thoughts, feelings, and actions are powerhouses for electricity to flow. Our will and intention direct the electrical currents as we see fit. This is why it is important to work on our beliefs and feelings. We are redirecting the flow. Forgiveness makes room for our energy to flow and creates space for our desire and imagination to expand in the direction of calmer waters where we can live with authenticity.

We always have free will and choice. Choose to do the work, clear the way, bring things to consciousness and discover the power of choice. As they say in the twelve step programs, "Take what you like, and leave the rest." When the intention is there and the student is ready, the teacher appears. You are your ultimate best teacher to guide your life. If you take nothing else, please hear this: Listen to your own wisdom, and try some of these processes out. Keep sailing my friends.

The Artist now has all the materials to create from: desire, intention/decision, imagination and expectation. Now, let's do some exercises to help solidify all these fresh and positive choices into our lives.

EXERCISES:

STUCK VISIONS/STUCK BELIEFS

This exercise is ideal if you are feeling stuck in negative beliefs. It can also be used to reframe these beliefs, images or thoughts you have discovered from the content in this chapter.

1. Choose a situation where you feel stuck.

2. Listen to the inner dialogue that goes with it. For example: *I am sitting in my driveway thinking I never should have moved. I hate this new house.*

3. Imagine the situation as clearly as you can. Rebuild the image in your mind with all your senses, smell what it is like in the car, hear the sounds, notice how the air feels on your skin, look at what is in front of you as if you are there now.

4. What are you thinking? *I hate this new house. I hate myself for saying "yes" to moving.*

5. What would you like to know instead? This new thought needs to be something you are willing to say "yes" to. You can't change your past but you can change your relationship to it and how you live, because of your thoughts. A new thought might be: *I am grateful for what brought us here, and I love and appreciate myself for following my decision. I am happy here and appreciate myself for being part of the decision.*

6. Now, imagine yourself in that moment as if it is now. Rebuild it with the new thought going through your head, but everything else is the same. You are sitting in

the car looking in the same direction seeing the same thing but the resulting thoughts have changed.

7. Notice how you feel in your body and in that moment.

8. When you are ready to finish, slowly look around your location, breathe deeply and stretch your body. Be aware of the day, the time and the place you are in. Squeeze your arms. Gently rub your head and shoulders. Complete the exercise as you need to.

9. Revisit this new image in your daily meditation practice. Over time it will replace the old.

INTENTION SETTING

Use this approach for any task you are setting out to do, or a thought you want to change or to simply start your day.

For example:

1. State what you want to shift, such as shifting a strong belief you have been carrying which blocks you from getting a certain job: *I am not good enough.*

2. What is the motive to change it, and what is the hesitation/resistance/conflict around changing it? *I feel it has not served me, and there is a part of me that is scared to shift because that is the only way I know life—yet I want to and am willing to take steps toward it.*

3. State clearly your intention to shift. *I am willing to change my thinking around not being good enough.*

4. From here you will start to notice this willingness to go from "I am not good enough" to "I am good enough" (or even more, depending on how far you are willing to set your intention and live up to it. Take

it step by step). This will bring new opportunities to you. Internally, you may experience it as being guided to certain people, places or things. Sometimes your intention may appear blocked, yet your ability to discover where you are stuck is still part of the manifesting process. Working through being stuck can lead to the name of a therapist, healer, coach, or place of worship to support you. Or, you may start to go to the doctor, gym, shift eating patterns, to name a few ways we shake free on the way to manifesting our intentions. All these things can occur because you set your intention and desire in a new direction. Great work, Captain!

RECEIVING POSITIVE COMMENTS

1. Ask people you know who care about you to tell you things they like/love about you.
2. Write them on a Post-it.
3. Stick the Post-it around in your house.
4. Each time you pass it, repeat what it says and then move it so every time you walk by it, it is fresh and new. If you don't move it over time you will walk right past it because you saw it there before.
   a. When someone says something nice to you repeat the words to yourself like the most delicious piece of food you ever tasted. Then slowly take it into your entire body imagining it going through your entire digestive track. Release what you do not want, and let the remainder become part of

your circulatory system. Receive it into every cell of your body where you want it. Feel the warmth, the love, the compassion of this statement and the love from the person.

b. Look in the mirror, into your eyes, repeat a phrase or two and see what it is like to receive your own words as if you are speaking to your best friend.

SWITCHING LITTLE VOICES

This is ideal for any thought patterns that no longer serve you. I have separated the meditation process out into a separate exercise because you can also use it to work with any other thoughts where you feel conflict—besides a little voice pulling you away from your positive intention.

A physical exercise that goes along with the releasing your inner "No" is: Becoming Free. www.cynthasis.com/the-curious-voyage-resources/ (Do not do this or any exercise without first checking with your doctor. Adapt all instruction to your physical comfort, and do at your own risk).

1. Think of the little voice that says some version of "No.": *I don't want to do this. It's stupid. I can't ... I am not capable. How come it has to be like that?*

It may sound much like a child's or adolescent's voice. For example: you are about to start a new exercise program but you think: *Maybe tomorrow, or what is the point?*

2. Write down the thoughts and any stories you have in relation to them.

3. Notice your energy as you are thinking about them.

4. Is your body getting tense?

5. Scan your body from the top of your head to the tips of your toes and notice any tension. Take note of it.

6. How does the tension manifest? Is there any connection between the tension and the "No" voice? Does it feel like the "No" voice is weighing you down or blocking you from moving? Watch out for the answer to this question being "No." The "No" voice may be very good at helping you think there is nothing wrong with not doing what you set out to do. For example, if you are starting a new exercise program it may tell you this is not the time, because you have too much work to do. Doing work may sound responsible, but it is really just an excuse to not start the new pattern of exercising. You may need to open your mind to discovering things different than you have up to now as you are shaking an established pattern.

7. How is your breathing being affected now as you are doing this process?

8. Notice.

9. Take a moment to do some drawing, move your body or whatever you need to do to feel and hear the negative voices expressing themselves. Sometimes putting on hard drumming music helps to get you moving.

10. Often the "No" voices are a form of fear talking. You can work with it using the Meditation Using Three Voices Exercise that follows—or for now, simply notice and journal about it.

MEDITATION USING THREE VOICES

This three-part process connects with aspects of the self, one at a time. It has helped many people overcome confusion, obsessive thinking, worrying, emotional reactions, anxiety and personal/interpersonal conflicts. I was originally introduced to this process through the Pathwork, a self-growth, self-transformation process. This process is on YouTube at: https://youtu.be/7eeEfxdt640.

1. Find a comfortable spot and set some time aside. It is best to have a journal or paper to write on, because writing creates movement, change and transformation out of our original thought—or the loopy thinking we can get caught in.

2. Notice the part of you that has decided to do this, and even found this tool to explore, is your healthy ego. It is the executor in you that makes decisions, sets time aside, and follows through. It is the part of you that observes, gets curious and wants to know.

   a. Take note that you are asking for help with this thought, conflict, fear and/or "No" voice. I will use the example of wanting to start a new exercise program.

   b. Define the conflict clearly: *I would like help with the part of me that keeps putting off my desire to exercise.*

   c. Notice how you are stuck with the conflict: *I want to, but I never get around to it.*

   d. How has this affected your life? *I am feeling sluggish, falling into old patterns of not wanting to do much, a little depressed, bloated, irritable.*

e. What inner conflicts are you now living with because you may be following a rule from your rulebook that relates to this issue? *The rule in my family has been that work comes first, so now I have no time to exercise. There also has been a rule to be healthy so not sure how I can do both which is making me feel worse about myself. It is a downward spiral. I just want to veg out.*

f. Notice this inner conflict has two opposing forces. Part of you wants something different. *I want to feel better, but I feel overwhelmed with everything I have to do.*

g. The conflict may have been showing up in your life as frustration, anger, depression, anxiety, to name a few ways. *Feeling more depressed and not as good as other people. I am comparing myself more and feeling more lethargic. I don't want to do things I normally think are fun.*

h. However conflict has appeared, think of it as a part of you that has not had a need met, been understood or heard. For this process think of it as a part of you that is younger than your present age. *I am feeling like a young adult who is overwhelmed.*

i. It may want something from the other person, something that is less authentic, honest or straightforward, or it could be that it does not want to follow some rule or requirement (could be it just doesn't want to get out of bed and go to work), feels angry, mad, scared, sad, self-righteous, bullied, or thinks it knows what is best for you and in some way, even thinks it is protecting you. In fact, it may have been very useful at some point, but it is no longer needed as often or in the same way.

j. Take time to hear what this part is: *Frustrated part that is just fed up with life.*

k. Observe its thoughts, feelings and actions: *Sad, lonely, disappointed.*

l. Ask it what it wants: *A vacation.*

m. Ask it what it needs: *Time.*

n. Keep looking at it, observing it and hearing it: *As I keep listening, I hear that it wants alone time and a sense of connection with nature.*

o. Thank it for sharing this information with you: *Thank you, Self, for sharing.*

3. Turn toward your wise inner self/higher power/higher self/inner knowing, and ask for help with this part. It is important to not go into the hard, painful feelings and thoughts without support from the best in you. We all have a higher/best part that is ready, willing and able to assist, when we ask. This can also be the present day, strong, adult self that understands, has compassion and wisdom. We each refer to this part of ourselves in slightly different ways. If you need to, you can ask for support from your God, as you experience God. The key is that this part of you is different than the ego. It has that kind

of intuitive wise knowing that is beyond logical thinking. It can help when you feel stuck.

4. Let a conversation open up between the "unmet need self" and the "wise part." This is not a fix-it conversation, but a willingness to sit and listen and have love toward the part of you that feels its needs are unmet.

5. Wait and see what happens when truth meets pain and confused thinking: *As I kept asking it what it needed, I felt less identified with it and felt like my higher self was the part asking the young adult what she needed. This helped me start to feel more compassion and shifted me away from frustration.*

Let's try this with some of the rules we spoke of earlier. *I am supposed to be with family this weekend, but I don't want to go.*

Key words are: "supposed to." So, if you are in a conflict and you hear "should have," "would have," "could have," or "supposed to" but don't want to, it is helpful to do this process.

1. Decide to take this upsetting decision into the meditation process.

2. State what the issue is. *I don't really want to go, but I know I should.*

3. Listen to that part of you that is saying "no" to going. That part may say: *My values say "go" because it is family, and my feelings say "no" because they are all hypocrites. They lie and cheat each other. They are so fake.* Let that voice that says "no" to going continue to express itself.

4. You may feel overwhelmed on how to resolve this, and that is a good time to turn to the wiser voice.

5. Speak and invite the wiser voice to come in: *I need your help. I hear all these negative thoughts. I feel the anger and am stuck.*

Often the state of stuck is because we feel that "child part" or because we were never allowed to follow our own voice. This wise voice will go beyond the words and further into the feelings. It may ask:

When you realize they are fake and hurtful:

1. *What happens to you?*
2. *What do you want from this?*
3. *What do you need?*
4. *What do you really need?*

At some point the part that does not want to go, calms down and there often is a deep inner connection.

As stated earlier, we can't change others but we can change the way we respond to a situation, or our habitual perspective, and we can soothe our inner parts that were originally wounded. From there we can make wiser choices of how we want to approach the situation.

The above exercise also gives us a deeper understanding of whatever our issue is. It can be used to help us set a new course.

START DIGGING INTO WHAT YOU DESIRE AND YOUR INTENTION

Desire is a longing for what you truly want.

Intention is what you are willing to put your action behind to bring about your desire.

So, ask yourself these questions:

1. *What games did I enjoy playing?*
2. *How did my playful activities match my desires?*

3. *What do I want?*

4. *What do I need?*

5. *What do I truly desire?*

The other question around desire to consider is: *What percentage of me feels my energy is behind this desire?*

If you respond with less than 80 percent, explore deeper what you really need to help you believe in your desire.

Ask: *What is stopping me from aligning with this desire?*

What am I willing to move, shift, change to help make this desire stronger?

You may want to do some Self-Spotting on this. (See Chapter 1)

Once you have a really strong sense of your desire, move to the following Set Your Intentions Exercise.

SET YOUR INTENTIONS

This exercise will help you set your course with focus and purpose. Intention is a key ingredient for manifestation. You want to first align with the energy that supports your values so you can create your desire.

1. Think of what it is you would like to create. For example: *I want to expand my business.*

2. How is that in alignment to your values? *I'm shy, so not really.*

3. What are the characteristics you now possess to help you manifest that desire, and what characteristics do you need to strengthen to create this? For example, *I may want to expand my business but I really feel shy and resist*

networking. I need to first work on my shyness to help strengthen my energy to be in alignment with my intention.

4. How ready are you to manifest this in your life and set your intention for it to happen? If the answer is 80 percent or more go to Question 6. If it is less, explore questions 3-5.

5. What is stopping you?

6. What next steps do you need to take to help you set the intention?

7. What characteristics do you want to align with to help you get to your desired creation?

8. Can you make the intention different to fit those next steps?

9. Are you having any internal negative self-talk that is making this hard to manifest? For example: *I want to switch my career. Yet, I don't see how that is possible.* What in my rulebook says I can't? Use the exercises in Chapter 2 to help you with these rules.

10. Create a mental image for your desire. See it as an actual scene you are in much like a movie scene. Bring life to it. Imagine it, desire it and expect it is already so.

Below we break down how to work with your imagination and expectations to support your intention.

VISUALIZATION INTO A NEW STATE

This exercise will help you expand into a new way of being. Keep a journal as you articulate your thoughts.

1. Do your own research by observing other people who have aspects you would like to emulate or the

life you would like to have. If you can see it in them then there must be some part of you that has it too—otherwise you would probably not notice or be interested in those attributes. A teacher once taught me that we are only jealous of the things we *can* have for ourself.

2. Once you finish your research and have a sense of what you wish for and can see it more clearly, start to build it.

    a.   What is the vibration of the characteristic, the lifestyle? What body posture do you take on when living this way? What color, sound, smell and/or flavor represents it?

    b.   What is a day like in that life?

    c.   If you enjoy art projects, create something that represents this life.

Vision boards are great outlets to reflect and express. They can take on a power of their own. One time I did a vision board and ended up moving into a house with the same countertop that was on the vision board. I never thought of countertops as a real concern or need. It was a "coincidence." I also noticed over time I got some form of everything on the board.

Nightly Gratitude

Make a brief list of what makes you feel grateful. You may need to start with thinking of three people you are grateful for each night to get your mind moving in the right direction. If that is too challenging, start with things instead of people, but research has shown that gratitude journaling tends to be more effective when participants focus on gratitude for people rather than material objects. Take time to savor each blessing, and remain open to surprises.[12]

CLEARING PRIDE, SELF-WILL AND FEAR

This exercise can help you become conscious of how these three primary faults impact a situation and/or relationship. Use it when you feel stuck in a pattern, mood or relationship. Use writing or talking out loud to help you get clarity and shift your thoughts and energy.

1. Pride
   a. What is your pride? How do you wish or see the other person(s) as not as good as you think they should be?
   b. How do you justify yourself in the situation?
   c. What do you think is wrong with the situation or the other person(s)?
   d. How could you do this better?
   e. How are you comparing yourself to the situation or the other person(s)? Are you better or worse?
   f. Do you feel competitive?
   g. Does that person remind you of someone? Are you better or worse?
2. Self-will
   a. What are your demands or expectations in this situation?
   b. What are you resisting giving up about your position?

    c. What do you keep asking for? When we ask repeatedly or keep trying that is actually a form of control. If you are holding on to control, you may be trying to push your will on the other person(s).

3. Fear

    a. How are you afraid in this situation?

    b. What are you not getting or asking for because fear says not to ask?

    c. What is the dialogue fear is speaking to you?

    d. What is the belief behind your fear statements?

    e. What rule in your rulebook are you acting from?

    f. What value are you afraid to live by because things won't work out the way you want?

You may want to do some journaling or meditating to get to the origin of this pattern. This may need some outside support and help to uncover and release.

We will expand on Pride, Self-will and Fear in Chapter 4.

[4]

GETTING CURIOUS ABOUT ENERGY AND LOVE

IF YOU LIVE AN AUTHENTIC LIFE, you will be happy and feel vital.

By now you have begun to see how we operate on automatic pilot much of the time. As a result, you understand why we act the way we do. As you have expanded your awareness of your patterns, you have gained freedom to approach life situations more authentically—and even to have more physical energy. It is possible to enhance this vital energy, called our life force, even further. It is available to all of us without limitation.

LIFE FORCE

We all have a life force, which we constantly use, either consciously or unconsciously. How we choose to use it is like the sculptor who takes a block of clay and creates a masterpiece. We also can take our life force energy, get to know it, and create a magnificent life.

Energy is the creative force that gives life to the whole universe. It is the vibration of all potential and possibility. By expanding our consciousness, we are better able to connect with this energy. When we connect consciously, our experience of life expands, and we give back to life far more readily and easily. This is what it means to participate in the flow of life for the greater good.

Humans are designed with certain energy centers in the body which convert, assemble and balance the flow and power of life force energy. These centers are connected to our endocrine system, which influences our moods. Clearing our energy centers enhances our flow and improves our mood. This amplifies our self-expression, freeing us to live a more authentic life.

Dr. John Pierrakos' book, *Core Energetics: Developing the Capacity to Love and Heal,* explores this dynamic, describing how opening our bodies to energy techniques shifts our mental state into a more powerful, loving one. Pierrakos, who founded Core Energetics, details how our energy centers may have been wounded during childhood. He reviews certain body structures based on wounding at various stages of development. He has determined that the front of the body is connected to our feelings, while the back connects directly to our will and intention.

BREATH

Our breath is one of the most accessible ways we amplify our life force. It is a vital function that is both conscious and unconscious. For thousands of years people have been focusing on the breath as a way to regulate the body and expand our energy centers, now commonly known as chakras. When we breathe shallowly and rapidly through our mouths it prevents proper air circulation throughout the body. In contrast, deeper, longer breaths through the nose help regulate your body.

Just the act of breathing through the nose provides numerous incredible health benefits. These include triggering the release of hormones into our bodies, expanding our lung capacity, increasing blood flow, raising oxygen intake, lowering blood pressure, relaxing our muscles, moderating our heart rate, improving deeper, restful sleep, and even storing more memories.[9]

A daily routine that includes focusing our breath creates a conscious habit out of what can be unconscious and automatic. When we bring awareness to our breath—exploring it and playing with it—we learn to align with our authentic, relaxed, healthy, balanced self. Yoga teaches many various breathing exercises. At the end of this chapter try the Brain/Body Connection Power and Breath to Connect Love and Power Exercises for more exploration of your own breath.

The essence of our vitality, or life force energy, can be defined with three primary attributes: love, power and serenity.

Choosing Love or Fear

Fear keeps us stuck in our patterns and becomes so familiar we can forget there's an alternative. As we move out of old habits, we sometimes feel lost. I speak to clients about this part of the voyage as feeling grief. This is natural. Stay alert, and continue to choose love.

Many teachers say every decision comes down to the choice between love and fear. Of course, we also can assign fear a bad rap. Fear serves an important purpose. Pema Chödron describes it this way: "Fear is a natural reaction to moving closer to the truth."

Here is an example of getting caught up in an old, fearful pattern and then choosing love instead:

I was having negative thoughts about a loved one who, in my opinion, was ruining their life. These thoughts came up out of nowhere, after I had a number of calm, relaxing days. The thoughts had a familiar ring, sounding just like my old rulebook, filled with judgments about others. I had been sailing in new waters of love and enjoyment. Then, without realizing it, I started to go fishing in old familiar territory.

I quickly became short-tempered, distant, and started justifying reasons to avoid my loved one. Then I caught a mental glimpse of myself, and realized my inner judgment was creating disconnection. My inner observer and narrator intervened with a question, "Wait, how is this helping your heart stay open?" This question is a good one, because I have a core value of remaining open.

I made a choice in that moment to stop thinking about my loved one's shortcomings and shifted my mental focus back to myself. I did some self-reflection about the feelings and thoughts the situation was stirring up inside of me. When I took ownership of my responses to them, it released my stuck energy of judgment and dissociation, raising my vibration. That is the power of love.

Love is a choice and a permanent force that does not come and go like eros, according to Dr. John Pierrakos. In *Eros, Love & Sexuality: The Forces That Unify Man and Woman*, he clearly differentiates between the two ideas. Eros is something powerful that many of us fleetingly experience. On the other hand, the experience of love can be cultivated and strengthened for a lifetime. It is a state of being when we drop our defenses, making us vulnerable—and in some cases, triggering old wounds. So, if we are feeling triggered by someone, or even an act of love, go within and get curious about your reaction. Turning within to find the inevitable cause rather than projecting your pain onto someone else is a transformative act of love for everyone involved.

LOVE AND COMPASSION

The Dalai Lama states, "Love and compassion are necessities, not luxuries. Without them, humanity cannot survive."

There is also an old Amish proverb that says, "Instead of putting others in their place put yourself in their place." Becoming more aware of what life is like from another person's point of view, helps us open our hearts and minds.

As a therapist I am often asked, "How can you listen all day long to other people's suffering?" Many people feel my clients' pain is burdensome to me. However, I have found the key to retaining my own sense of balance and ease is for me to listen with love. Listening in this particular way is the essence of compassion.

Recent research shows that there is a difference between compassion and empathy. When you feel empathy for another you put yourself emotionally in the other person's situation and feel what you perceive they may feel. As a result, you can get lost in those feelings. In contrast, compassion is the ability to feel for another, rather than as another, maintaining loving detachment, with the desire to help ease their suffering.

> PAUSE: Compassion activates the parts of our brain that are connected to love.

Compassion studies have shown it literally changes our brains. One such study found: "Compassion expands the love centers in your brain ... a short-term compassion training of several days can foster positive feelings and related brain activations, even when persons are exposed to the distress of others."[10]

After sharing the difference between empathy and compassion with a client, she had an aha! moment. With eyes wide open in wonder she asked, "You mean I don't have to do everything for everyone if it is overwhelming to me?" No, you don't.

There are times we can say "no" to other people's needs and still be very compassionate toward them. In other words, we can detach from their experience, and still be loving. In Al-Anon, this is very accurately referred to as "detaching with love." I can love someone, and feel for them, but I don't have to take on what they are experiencing for myself.

The American political arena has been very challenging and divisive. Practicing meditations on compassion is extremely helpful during these times to help us keep an open heart. The Compassion Institute (https://

community.compassioninstitute.com) has great courses, and some practices can be found at: www.cynthasis.com/the-curious-voyage-resources/.

However you develop and enhance compassion, it will lead you to an infinite, creative force of life.

POWER

> *Be the change that you wish to see in the world.*
> —Mahatma Gandhi

Choose to align your power with love! Be the change! You have the power. How do you use it? You are the Captain. It is a powerful force to feel the connection to love with others. It is a force we can grow with as we expand our vitality.

CONNECTING POWER AND LOVE

I have seen leaders connect to their followers and feel a mutual loving connection with them. Unfortunately, sometimes a leader is infused with so much energy that their ego can't tolerate it. This can lead to the misuse of power. Once this happens, the ego takes over and the followers can be taken advantage of—and may not even know it.

I have also seen an imbalance of power in loving relationships; especially when it comes to money. When one partner is solely responsible for controlling the shared money, at a certain point the love between them becomes lost. In that situation, power is experienced without love. Then the person controlling the money may even misuse it without any regret. The other person is often unaware of what is happening.

We can easily go astray when the ego is not grounded in the intention to love. All this is to say we benefit greatly by using our power with love. Grow into the expansion.

SERENITY

> *A voice inside the head says, "I know you're tired, but come.*
> *This is the way."*
> *—Rumi, The Essential Rumi*

Serenity is the state of saying "yes" to life. It is a sense of being calm, peaceful, untroubled, and in the flow of life's natural energy.

Brian, a prideful man who rarely asked for help, came to have sessions with me because he was feeling lost and overwhelmed by major changes at his work. His significant love relationship was doing well, but he was beginning to damage it. His stress at work was creating a situation where uncontrollably he was returning to old, destructive habits. The relationship was at risk. To save the relationship he cared deeply about, Brian found the courage to seek help. He surrendered to trust.

> *PAUSE: How often do we have choices to decide to go into the unknown and choose an uncertain path?*

We are now sailing in new waters. Just like Brian we can use our power to align with serenity and keep following our intention toward love. Brian gave over his fears and worries about work based on his old rulebook. As a result, he found himself making fresh choices out of love for himself and love for his partner.

A personal example of integrating love, power and serenity during some very stormy waters happened to me during and after a hurricane. I was visited early one morning by the fire department during a hurricane. They came to determine if I needed help, and after assessing all the houses on the flood-line I won the use of their pump. They informed me I needed to keep it running all day. But I was unable to get extra gas from the local gas station because the town had no electricity. As I tried to pass over to the next town the police informed me to stay home. I was in a quandary. How could I get gas to last all day if I couldn't get to a gas station? I had to surrender. In that surrender a few unexpected gifts appeared. The bridge I would have crossed was wiped out. I returned home safely to my dog, and strangers gifted me gas. I felt a deeper sense of connection.

Once that storm ended another one came. Neighbors told me that having an electric panel in a flooded basement was a hazard. Between broken windows, an electrical hazard and mold spreading, I felt overwhelmed. I was trying hard to save this house. My old rulebook dictated I ought to be kind to a landlord who never even came to check on the house or my safety during two hurricanes. His concern was solely the rent money. Fortunately, I was on a month-to-month lease.

After letting go of old beliefs and living in the now with self-compassion, power and serenity, I moved out the next weekend. As life would have it, a friend of mine who was a lawyer offered to help me stand up for my rights. Then another friend, who had just lost her tenant, offered her lower-level apartment to me. Serenity to the "what is" helped me realize why I didn't have to wait until Spring to move to Georgia.

I did not plan for all the details and had no idea when I could travel to find a place to live, but each day with serenity things came to be. I was in the flow, even in the midst of an actual hurricane. Don't get me wrong; I have done my time stuck in fear and worrying what others thought. Eventually I learned I could use my power for a greater good. By kindly and considerately supporting all those I was connected to, I opened a path for a smooth move. I am so grateful for everyone who supported that transition.

One amazing thing about all being connected is that as I met people in my new life in Atlanta many were connected to friends from years ago when I lived there in the 1990's. When we are in the flow, everything in our life is more connected. This is part of the infinity. It is what we live in when we are beyond practical thinking.

A daily routine of mindful awareness, meditation and exercise helps us get to this state of flow. There are many ways to meditate and exercise based on your natural rhythm and what helps you connect to this infinite soul-centric space.

CONNECTING TO SERENITY

At a certain point we realize all the thoughts and words we have simply will not express everything we wish to communicate. When that realization dawns, we go beyond our current state of awareness. We tap into something that is much more than our physical bodies and material world. We perceive a realm that is spacious, formless, unexpected—where all possibility exists and anything is possible. In this state of being we are beyond our thinking ego. Here we find a place of wonder and curiosity where we do not have to explain ourselves. Beyond any human comprehension we find ourselves surrounded simply by love and light. That is what it means to experience serenity in its purest sense.

The exercises below will help you experience your vitality and the exquisite experience of Love, Power and Serenity.

EXERCISES:

LOVE, POWER, SERENITY EXERCISE: RELEASING CAPES

These inquiry questions can help you explore other situations and shift the energy. They will expand on the Pride, Self-will and Fear Exercise from Chapter 3.

1. First, state the situation. For example, *thinking about what was wrong with the way a loved one is living their life.*

2. Next, what is your intention to create the best outcome in the situation? In the example, you may wish to *keep the love and connection open between the two of you.*

3. What belief/rule from your rulebook could you shift to help you align yourself better with your intention? In the example, *I have a belief/rule in the power of judging others and thinking I know what is best for the other person.*

4. Write down what your belief might be, and notice:

    a. Where is my willful demand that I be right, I be heard, I be seen and/or I be understood in this situation? How is it blocking me from having my intention materialize? In the example, *I noticed I was being irritable, short tempered, impatient and closed off.*

b. In what way may I be trying to force the other person to do things or see things my way? In the example, I *would be overly active in giving my opinion.*

c. How may I be withholding or withdrawing from the other person? Acts of withholding or withdrawing often indicate there is some kind of power struggle going on in the situation. If so, see what your part is and what you could surrender to create a positive shift. In the example, *I chose to surrender into trust. Not just for my partner, but to the larger idea that whatever happens to us as a couple is what is meant to be.* This is where serenity comes in, and a great tool to use for surrendering is the opening of the Serenity Prayer: *God grant me the serenity to accept the things I cannot change.* (I can't control another person's behavior. Feel free to replace the word 'God' with one that is more comfortable for you if you prefer.) *The courage to change the things I can.* (I stopped myself, became observant and chose to shift my thoughts and actions.) *And the wisdom to know the difference.* (I can't control the outcome by trying to get someone to be different.)

5. Visualization: Imagine you are at the edge of a lake. You are wearing three fine capes. They are the capes of pride, self-will and fear.

a. Cape of pride: This cape is designed with all the ways you are right—and ways you are better or worse than the other person.

b. Cape of self-will: It is sewn with all the ways you are forcing something in the situation so your way can win.

c. Cape of fear: This cape is filled with all the statements that make you think you can't let go of your position. It knows all the ways the other person is wrong and you are right. It is filled with beliefs about how you are better or worse and has you convinced this is the way it is and if you shift in any direction something bad will happen. You can't let go. Yet you long for your intention to set you free.

Freeing yourself into the lake of the unknown: As you imagine yourself standing there wearing these capes and looking into the water think of what you desire and long for. What is your intention? What do you imagine is possible for you? And, when you are ready, take off the capes one at a time and dive into the lake of the unknown and let your intuition and imagination show you the way.

The above is one of many ways to let go of our tight, dualistic thinking.

DANCING INTO LOVE

If you want to give birth to your true self, you are going to have to dig deep down into that body of yours and let your soul howl. Sometimes you have to take a leap of faith and trust that if you turn off your head, your feet will take you where you need to go.
—Gabrielle Roth

Another fun way to work with our energy is to dance it out. The dance described in this section can be done sitting or standing—whatever you are capable of doing. You can use your mind to imagine it. Visualization and movement have been found to help people heal from physical restrictions. It works similar parts of the brain.

Dance in whatever way is physically right for you. You may need to simply imagine the action of dancing or move your arms or feet and sway based on your physical ability.

1. Find a place that is private or comfortable for you to feel free to move.

2. Set an intention of what you want to dance toward. You may state something like:

    a. My intention is to release my judgments toward _____ and to open my heart to compassion.

    b. Or, my intention is to release the tension in my body that is blocking my peace in relation to _____. Or, my intention is to open to all possibilities to find _____. Choose something that has meaning to you.

    c. Turn on some drumming music. Various versions are found on YouTube, or choose a strong rhythmic beat that suits you. Let the beat impact your energy.

3. Start to move. See what happens.
4. Shift the music to other rhythms. Gabrielle Roth speaks of 5 rhythms in her movement video called The Wave, A Moving Meditation:
   a. Flowing (fluid movements)
   b. Staccato (short stops and starts)
   c. Chaos (wild and free)
   d. Lyrical (playful and light and will move to)
   e. Stillness (the still point of your moving center)
5. Create your own. Find a playlist that suits you. Notice how you feel now that you have moved your body.

Dance, movement (imagined or actual) and integrating our body into our awareness will shift us to a deeper connection to self.

Dance up your inner family and shift internal relations.

You can do this by putting on some music that has a masculine tone, a feminine tone, a playful tone and then dancing the integration of the masculine/father energy, the feminine/mother energy and the playful child energy. Let the inner family integrate, shift, move, heal and fall in love with each other.

Brain/Body Connection Power

A basic point of entry, exit and regulation is our brainstem. Here we have parts of our brain that support our respiration, circulation, balance, digestion and much more. It is a pathway for our nerves to go from our brain to our body and back again.

Connecting the two:

1. Get comfortable in a seated position.
2. Place one hand gently on top of your head and the other at the base of your skull and neck.
3. Breathe and notice.
4. Let your eyes gaze at a spot or close your eyes and follow your breath and rhythm.
5. Notice what happens. Switch hands when ready.
6. Take a deep breath and notice how you feel.

BREATH TO CONNECT LOVE AND POWER

This exercise will open up your body and support the connection between love and power. Perform these movements based on your physical ability. Imagine, sit or lie down. Do not continue if you are finding the breath creating anxiety versus joy. Sometimes full breathing can present a nervousness and activate old pain you are needing to approach with professional help. If this happens seek help to work with breath in a therapeutic environment.

1. Put one hand on your heart and one on your lower belly. If you are lying down bend your knees.
2. Breathe in and feel the air going into your lower belly pushing your lower hand up then your upper hand. Let your head stretch back and your chest expand.
3. Gently press (so you are aware you are releasing first from your chest then your lower belly) with your upper hand as you breathe out. Curl your shoulders with your head

tucked in. Suck in with your lower belly as you continue to exhale.

4. Wait until ready to take the next breath and do it again.
5. Each time feeling your hands.
6. Now breathe in again expanding your chest and exhale contracting.
7. If you feel a lot of excitement tap, stamp or shake your legs to release the energy.
8. Let out a sigh or any other sound to open your chest.
9. Keep breathing and bring your awareness into your heart, lower belly and back sensing you are connected within. Feel strong, vital and loved.

COMPASSION

This exercise is ideal to pause and connect to a state of love.

1. Breathe deeply with one or two hands on your heart.
2. Think and/or feel compassion for yourself.
3. Speak out loud 3 times: *I am safe. I am kind. I am whole. I am love.*
4. Now think of someone you love, and state 3 times: *You are safe. You are kind. You are whole. You are love.*
5. Now think of someone you are challenged by. Speak out loud 3 times: *You are safe. You are kind. You are whole. You are love.*
6. Now think of your community. Speak out loud 3 times: *We are safe. We are kind. We are whole. We are love.*
7. Now think of the world. *We are safe. We are kind. We are whole. We are love.*

There are various exercises on developing compassion as it is a state of being to develop. https://zenhabits.net/a-guide-to-cultivating-compassion-in-your-life-with-7-practices/.

[5]

INTUITION AND RECEPTIVITY

WE STARTED OUR JOURNEY on automatic pilot. Then we took the helm ourselves by assessing our priorities and exploring our beliefs. From there we tuned into our bodies for better guidance, and we activated the energies of love, power and serenity to steer us. We are ready to expand our connection to intuition and receptivity. These two states of being support our authenticity and strengthen our connection to ourselves and to others.

INTUITION

Intuition is the ability to understand something immediately without a reasonable explanation. Malcolm Gladwell addresses this in *Blink* where he shows how "fast and frugal" thinking is more accurate than heavily analyzed data. Intuitive thinking is an ability we all have.

PAUSE: Write down some key intuitive moments you had this week.

One day I was kayaking and wanted a swim before leaving the area. However, back at the car the mood had left me entirely—it seemed even my body was disinterested. I listened to how I was feeling. As we drove home a bad storm rolled in. It would have overrun and endangered us if we had lingered to swim. I felt such gratitude for listening to an inexplicable feeling without questioning it.

We were born as sensitive, self-attuned beings. The more conscious we become and trust our bodies rather than follow the rulebook, the more we can fine-tune our own intuition.

Sometimes when we are anxious, it can be our intuition speaking, and should not be dismissed out of hand. Anxiety can be either intuition or fear. We can learn the difference by getting curious and listening to our bodies. I had exactly this sort of powerful intuitive experience taking the train into New York City to teach. I had a bad case of nerves because this time I was teaching a new topic. The nerves quickly turned into an anxiety attack—which I had never experienced before. However, I managed to get through the worst of it and make it to class.

Once I arrived at class, however, I had some very challenging students. They constantly questioned me and my co-teacher about almost everything we were covering. They expressed anger and dissatisfaction and even began questioning the way the organization ran the program. It was one of the hardest groups I ever had to teach. Although they were all adults, they acted very immature and disrespectful. The entire experience showed me that my anxiety was really intuition. My body was giving information that was beyond conscious awareness.

DEVELOPING INTUITION

You can develop your intuition with more body awareness. You can also practice various exercises to become more attuned to your environment and others. Whatever you choose to do, expect to give it time to develop. Practice activities like meditation, journaling, dream journaling, and becoming curious about whatever captures your attention. Intuition can start small, like whispered thoughts that nudge you toward your next action. That little voice is worth listening to. See where it leads.

There have been a number of times where I did not listen to my intuition. I heard my whispering inner voice, but I reasoned it away. These situations left me with more problems than successes.

I have become much better able to hear my own intuition over time, doing all the things described so far in this book. I am better able to become still and listen for it from a place of trust. My intuitive voice has become stronger than my ego voice, which trusts logic and forgets that I am connected to a wiser voice within.

It didn't start that way. I was one of those people who used to make deals with "God." For example, the day I locked the keys in the car I told God, "If you help me get them out, I promise not to be mean to myself anymore." Then there was the day I did not listen to the voice that said, "Don't lose the bike lock key"—and I did it anyway. I ended up having to go to the welder to have the lock cut off because the locksmith could not help.

Look at those last two examples. Keys are a common theme for me. Our intuition often shows up in these common thematic and highly symbolic ways. When we see them, we can explore and find even deeper meanings.

PAUSE: What ways has your intuition been showing up lately?

Part of tuning into our intuition is tuning into our body, its senses and gentle nudges—or electrical impulses. We can develop this body insight with some of the exercises from previous chapters, especially Chapter 2, with the Ball of Light, and in Chapter 4, Dancing into Love, Brain/Body Connection Power, and Breath to Connect Love and Power. Each of these helps charge up our bodies and support our connectedness to everyone and everything.

As we develop our intuition, we become more receptive to its wisdom, voice and energy. This is the attribute of receptivity.

RECEPTIVITY

When I shared about the storm from my kayak adventure, I described my own receptivity. I had no idea how that day was going to turn out logically. Fear kept coming and going, yet I stayed open to what was being presented to me—like the fire department showing up and offering me a pump to remove the water from the basement. They also helpfully informed me that I was living right on a flood line. The police were also present, helping me with the directive to go home and not cross a bridge to get gas. Additionally, there were friends helping me keep the pump going and providing me with shelter and food. At the end of the day the water receded, and the flood left.

Receptivity is our willingness to be open. When one person is willing to be open and receptive, they allow someone else the opportunity to give. This giving and receiving is an endless cycle, connecting all of us. We referenced this when we discussed all those who helped bring this book into being. Now we get to return to this idea with playful curiosity.

Receptivity is part of the natural rhythm of life, and it is influenced by our brainwaves—the electrical signals our neurons have when communicating with each other. The more receptive we are, the more we are in the flow of life, experiencing a state of calm and resiliency—and our hearts feel more open.

We can actually understand this better through exploring how brainwaves work. Brain waves and brain activity can be measured on an EEG (electroencephalogram). The EEG pattern appears as waves when it is recorded. There are five distinct brainwaves we can measure with the EEG: gamma (awake, alert and very focused attention) to beta (awake and alert) to alpha (calm relaxed not concentrating on anything too much) to theta (relaxed) to delta (deep sleep/relaxing state where internal healing can occur).

Besides measuring them, we can also shift our brain waves in various ways. One such way is Brainspotting. Another is an instrument called the Alpha-Stim. Many of my clients have found it very effective. The Alpha-Stim is an FDA-approved electrotherapy device which is designed to aid in healing insomnia, depression and anxiety. Believe it or not, there are also various phone apps that can help alter brain waves.

There are also low-tech approaches. Science has shown, as written in Healthline.com, "Relaxation techniques like mindfulness and meditation may help increase your alpha waves. This, in turn, may help you feel calmer, less anxious, and, according to some studies, may even boost your creativity level."

Regardless which brainwave altering approach you choose to explore, you are likely to find your "receptivity rhythm" is amplified and enhanced.

Another rhythm to focus on is sound. Music is a great way to flow with the rhythm of life—as is nature. Nature is filled with many layers of sound.

The world is never quiet when we really listen. Today I took a break and went for a hike in the woods. It was such a peaceful forest filled with life, radiating all kinds of sound rhythms from the water, to birds and the gentle breeze rustling the leaves. Then, looking up at the trees with deep contemplation, I could almost hear them talking. Perhaps this is why forest bathing is becoming so popular. One day it may even become as popular as yoga. Whether you call it bathing or not, I would highly recommend it to clear the mind, alter your own rhythms, open your heart and increase creativity.

Sound healing has actually been around for thousands of years. The ancient Greeks used sound healing to heal mental illness. Throughout history sound has been known to help improve morale, influence productivity, and heal the body.

In Brainspotting we use sound alternating between the right and left hemisphere to help deepen the healing process. Sound healing tools include gongs, tuning forks, singing bowls and much more. These various modalities can shift the brain wave frequencies going from beta to alpha to theta to support deep relaxation and healing.

The vestibulocochlear nerve in the ear connects to the vagus nerve. The vagus nerve, in turn, is key for much of our health and balance. It is correlated with capacity to regulate stress responses and can be influenced by breathing, its increase through meditation and yoga likely contribute to resilience and the mitigation of mood and anxiety symptoms.[11]

Once again, our body, mind and spirit are all connected in a beautiful rhythm.

Keep tuning in to the rhythm of life.

EMBRACING RHYTHM

Our brain wave state has a profound effect on us individually and in our relationships. Our vibration is felt within and all around us. One company that has a tool to measure frequencies among individuals, couples and groups is HeartMath. They have shown that the emotional state is encoded in the magnetic field within the heart and emanates through the environment attracting or repelling others. This all happens below our conscious awareness.

As you become familiar with your own rhythm and vibration you will become sensitive to the times when you get thrown off course and will steer yourself back from troubled waters. At the end of this chapter is an exercise to support you staying on course and shifting your personal vibrations.

PLAYING IN THE UNIVERSE

Knowing you are responsible for your actions, choices and frequencies which go along with your priorities and values, play and dance with all possibility. There are no boundaries. Sit in the open, still, endless sea and stay curious. Feel its own gentle rhythm. Enjoy the symphony and synchronicity of life. The surprises are endless and truly wonderful.

EXERCISE:

LISTENING

Practice listening and being. This will help you develop a different way of being with sound and vibrations for increasing your intuition.

1. Find a comfortable position to be for the next five minutes.
2. Gently close your eyes.
3. Notice the sounds around you.
4. Wait, and simply notice.
5. As thoughts arise, see them going past, like waves. Do not grab onto any thought, and if you do, simply come back to listening.
6. Notice the sounds outside you.
7. Pick one and observe it much like you were listening to a song. When your mind wanders pick another sound and do the same.
8. After three sounds, choose to notice your sounds. Notice your breath.
9. Listen to any other sounds you experience within.

10. Simply listen and when you feel ready, gently open your eyes.

In this space of conscious listening, notice what it is like to receive and listen to others without an agenda and without needing to add anything but your presence.

[6]

DESTINATION AUTHENTICITY

CONGRATULATIONS, Curious Captain!

The voyage you started here is one of endless discovery. Curiosity will keep you amazed. Keep your awareness, love, power and serenity in the forefront.

You are not alone. We said at the beginning of our voyage, and we say now, "No man is an island unto himself." Countless people, just like you, reading this book for the first time, have become aware of their strengths and weaknesses, have shed their rulebook and are sailing with more freedom and creativity. You are on a journey toward your authentic life, filled with vibrancy, peace, connection, creativity, love, purpose, passion and freedom!

This book is meant to be used in an ongoing basis, not just once. The tools here can be used repeatedly, and each time you will have a different experience. This is simply because as you grow you have new perspectives.

Keep doing the exercises. Set your intention on what you hope to gain. Let it guide you to unexpected places. Stay curious and keep growing. This is an endless process.

> *Sail away from safe harbor. Catch the wind in your sails. Explore.*
> *Dream. Discover.*
> *—Mark Twain*

NOTES

1. https://www.brucelipton.com/the-wisdom-your-cells/

2. https://www.wired.com/2014/12/your-atomic-self-how-your-breath-connects-you-to-universe/

3. https://www.scientificamerican.com/article/why-we-are-wired-to-connect/

4. https://helenair.com/lifestyles/health-med-fit/solid-objects-are-mostly-empty-space/article_32b70fa2-af9f-11e1-8062-001a4bcf887a.html

5. https://www.scientificamerican.com/article/mind-aglow-scientists-watch-thoughts-form-in-the-brain

6. https://brainspotting.com/wp-content/uploads/2018/02/Corrigan-and-Grand-2013-MedHyp80-759-766.pdf

7. https://www.cnn.com/2020/05/16/politics/obama-graduate-together-speech/index.html

8. Viktor Frankl https://www.brainpickings.org/2013/03/26/viktor-frankl-mans-search-for-meaning/

9. https://www.npr.org/sections/health-shots/2020/05/27/862963172/how-the-lost-art-of-breathing-can-impact-sleep-and-resilience.

10. https://www.sciencedirect.com/science/article/pii/S0960982214007702

11. https://www.ncbi.nlm.nih.gov/pmc/articles/PMC6189422/

12. Emmons& McCollough, 2003; Seligman, 2012;Seligman, et al., 2005).(https://files.eric.ed.gov/fulltext/EJ1112485.pdf)

ADDENDUM: EXERCISES

CHAPTER 1 EXERCISES

THE BREATH OF CONNECTION

1. Take a few deep breaths and get settled into a sitting position you can be comfortable in for five minutes. You may want to add some gentle music to this process.

2. As you breathe in and out, consider the air you are breathing is made up of atoms that have been around for thousands of years. Now consider this same air is part of what others are also inhaling and exhaling. The air is made of atoms that move around the Earth's atmosphere.

3. Continue to bring your awareness into your breath. Consider each breath is part of a larger atmosphere stretching beyond what you can sense.

4. Now, shift your awareness to your heart. As you feel it pumping blood throughout your body, consider the blood is made up mostly of water. The water surging through you right now is made of atoms that have been on the planet for centuries. These atoms in your blood contain hydrogen from an infinite universe and oxygen from the stars.

5. Experiencing this connection to the atoms, keep your awareness in your heart, and begin to imagine a yellow ribbon of light flowing out from your heart to the heart of someone you know. Imagine the ribbon then flowing out from that person's heart to someone else you both know. The ribbon continues on to someone that those two people know and then to someone you may not know but who lives in the neighborhood. This ribbon of light continues to flow, connecting to still others, multiplying connections, all the way around the globe.

6. You may not know all these individuals, but in this moment, consider how you are all connected. Keep breathing in and out, contemplating this sense of connection.

7. When you are ready, take out a journal/electronic note and write a little about your experience.

Although we may feel this state of connection from time to time, we often lose our awareness of it. Daily demands and habits interfere. However, as we dive into the topic of connection, taking the time to set aside the demands and habits that block us, we discover our authentic self, creativity and love.

SELF-SPOTTING: HEARING THE BODY

This can benefit you to shift from automatic pilot to awareness. It also can help when wanting to release pain in your body.

1. Take a moment to scan your body from the top of your head to the tips of your toes.

2. Find a spot in your body where you feel calm, grounded, and/or connected to your environment and/or inner self. See what that feels like. Spend some time feeling it, notice what it feels like in your muscles, on your skin, what the smells are around you as you focus on it. Breathe into it. Feel it.

3. Now, gently open your eyes and look around to find someplace that your eyes can relax as you keep feeling this calm, grounded, connected experience.

4. Keeping focusing and noticing.

5. Shift your body to expand into the feeling of being grounded and connected. You may want to tap your hands or feet or stretch a little or maybe rub your hands on the surface you are sitting on to really feel what it is you are connected with.

6. Relax and get into a position that will ensure your comfort, help you feel more relaxed. Get comfortable.

7. Sense/think/say to yourself: *I am here, I am present.*

8. Now, gently let your mind drift to a spot in your body that feels some tension/distress. Focus your attention there, without judgment or expectations. Notice this spot in your body as if you are saying: *Hello, I hear you. I see you.*

9. Try getting to know this spot. Does it have a color, a sound, a tone, a texture? If you could sense it like a part of you, speak to it: *Hello, _____. What is it you want to show me?* Keep your eyes on that calm, grounded spot you found in Step 2, as you connect with curiosity.

10. Let your mind wander and go wherever it needs to go. Now and then, check in with your calm, grounded spot

and the part of you that had the tension. Keep doing this for a while.

11. Focus on your breath. Is it shallow or deep? Feel what it is like to breathe in through your nose, then out through your mouth, with your exhale lasting a little longer than your inhale. If you are breathing comfortably through your nose, that is great. Keep going. Stay curious without forcing anything.

12. Remain curious, questioning and discovering whatever is happening and coming up.

13. Stay with it for as long as you like.

14. When you are ready to end, scan your body again and notice if there is a difference between the tension you started with and now. Is there a difference in how you feel toward the spot that was tense?

15. Take all the time you need and remember it is something to explore without judgment and expectations.

16. You are in a state of curiosity and wonder, a desire to hear from the stress part like a long-lost friend that has returned home.

17. Maybe ask this body part of yours to write or draw for you. Get to know it and what it may want to tell you. Be creative as you discover something new—or not. Remember, there are no expectations. Whatever comes up is exactly what comes up.

CONNECTING WITH VIBRATION: EXPLORING YOUR CURRENTS

As a reminder, we are all made of electrical currents. Let's work with this electricity and see how we can connect to ourselves as a reliable resource. Later we will be able to achieve even deeper dives into our subconscious and subcortical parts.

This helps to get settled into your energy and charge up if you are feeling a low vibration or to release if you are feeling too much vibration.

1. While doing this, put one hand on your stomach and one on your heart. Wiggle your toes a little. Settle into a seated or standing position.

2. Take a moment to take a few deep breaths—in through your nose and out through your mouth. As you breathe in, fill up your stomach, then your chest, and as you breathe out, empty your chest then your stomach.

3. Keep breathing in and out, noticing your hands moving up and down on your stomach and chest. Feel the air enter your nose and leave your mouth.

4. As your chest expands, let your shoulders go back, and as you exhale, let your shoulders move in ever so gently. This will build up a charge in your body. So as with an electric current, if we have an excess of charge, we need to discharge. As needed, let yourself loosen up some of the energy by shaking your arms and hands and tapping your feet on the ground.

5. Once you have discharged, you can do it again or just simply sit and breathe softly feeling the sensations in your body.

6. Notice how by using your breath and the air around you, you can shift your vibration.

7. If you want to continue, keep your focus on the vibration and gently close your eyes.

You Are Magnificent

This exercise is helpful for strengthening the connection to yourself without any negative thoughts, or to amplify positive ones. It may be hard to consider yourself as magnificent at first, so try it on. I have a friend who always addresses me, "Hello, beautiful." One day I was looking in the mirror with my usual self-talk and decided maybe I should say what she says to address myself. My way had not been helping me feel better. So, I started saying, "Hello, beautiful," to myself. The person in the mirror liked me better. Over time I realized why not keep doing it that way—because everything is subjective, and how I choose to see myself affects the reality I create? If I want to see myself as magnificent, people will also start to see me that way. So, let's give it a try.

1. Find a comfortable position. Take a few deep breaths.

2. As you breathe in and out, feel your back against the surface you are on. Feel your feet against the surface, and relax into your breath. Feel your level of relaxation grow with each breath.

3. Notice the air coming in and going out of your body, especially at the tip of your nose. Feel your chest and stomach rise and fall.

4. Now focus on your skin. Think of it, touch your hand and notice what it feels like. Is it hot, cold, or simply comfortable? Just notice, without judgment. As you feel and think about your skin, consider the pores of your skin. Your skin is the largest organ of your body. Consider how porous you really are.

5. As you breathe in and out, imagine opening up your awareness to how you are connected to all of this: your skin, the surface, your pores and everything your pores take in from your environment. Now, sense the temperature at the surface of your entire body. The pores keep opening up and taking in all that is around you. This connects you to the inside and outside of the surface of your skin. This opening and closing to the life within and around supports you in being connected to life, to all possibilities. You are connected. You are present with the fullness of life. You are magnificent and you are connected.

6. Hear/think the words: *You are magnificent.* Say it out loud: *You are magnificent.* Hear the words, open your mind and consider: *You are magnificent.*

7. Keep breathing in and out. Consider the words: *You are magnificent,* and this time repeat them with "I." *I am magnificent.* Say it out loud: "*I am magnificent.*"

8. Now say: "*I am connected, I am with the fullness of life. I am magnificent.*"

9. Keep doing this for as long as you like, and when you are ready to end the time, bring your focus back to your skin, sense the temperature, sense the texture.

10. Now notice. Notice your skin touching the cloth or the texture of the surface you are on.

11. Breathe in and out. Say the words: *I am here now. I am connected. I am with the fullness of life. I am magnificent.*

CHAPTER 2 EXERCISES

FINDING BELIEFS

This exercise will help you find some core beliefs.

1. For the next week, write a description of your day from waking up to sleeping. Note any problems, frustrations or challenging connections with people. Just a very short description is needed as we are looking for common themes/patterns to get to core beliefs that drive you. Example: *Woke tired today, did my meditation and exercised, felt happier, went to work and got into traffic. I hate traffic, can't stand having to sit still. Turned on some music, good sounds and got to office/school eager to start the new project/meet friends/ learn from____. Things moved fast and felt relatively okay. Not too bad. Came home and crashed.* Next day: *Woke, had strange dream, can't remember, no classes, watched TV, got bored, shot some hoops, felt better, hung with friends, not very eventful ...* Continue for a week.

2. Notice any themes that repeat from day to day. Even if you did not jot it down this week, something may come to mind as you are noticing and looking for patterns. As you review, look for phrases you use, moods, emotions, and/or encounters with people. In the example above, the theme may be about uneventful days.

3. Inquire on the theme. How often does this happen over the past several months/years? Where else have I noticed this theme/pattern? Has this been a family trait, a learned pattern from friends or relatives, a state of mind I have fallen into?

4. How does this serve me? I don't mean positively per se. Often when we continue to do things unconsciously, we may be gaining something from it, and at the same time, there is a price we are paying. For example, *as long as things are uneventful, I don't have to risk making mistakes.* We can then see that risking making mistakes is a fear-based thought. *The price I pay for this is having more adventures in my life, going after jobs or subjects of interest to me.*

5. When I follow these thoughts and these patterns: I feel sad/bored/happy/glad/apathetic/purposeless. All our attitudes will lead to feelings and actions. What feelings and actions does this belief bring to you? Reflect on these feelings and see if you can explore the feeling a little with a meditation.

6. Having sat with the feelings, what conclusions or new thinking have you discovered?

7. Having choice: Once you sat with and explored the feelings and the belief, is there anything about this belief /attitude you would like to be different?

PRIORITIES AND VALUES

Priorities and values are central to our sense of self and our self-esteem. This exercise is helpful for clarity on what matters most to us and how we want to be in life from our authentic self.

Start with some reflection.

1. What were your parents/primary caregivers' values around money? School? Work?
2. What were their values around religion? Tradition? Getting together with family and/or friends?
3. What were their thoughts and values around status?
4. From the above list, write which values you continue to live by yourself.
5. What were the values you grew up with around exercise? Was exercise competitive or for fun? Did you play competitive sports? What values did your family have around that?
6. What values did you learn regarding health? How often did you see doctors? Did you go to school when sick? Did your parents work when sick? How often did you have dental checkups? What type of food did you eat growing up? Did you have seated meals? Fast food dinners? Who cooked and prepared meals?
7. From these experiences, what values do you continue to put toward exercise and health?

Now that you have reflected on the values you grew up with, let's look further into things that impact you.

1. What are three things that make you happy? Sad? Laugh?

2. Who do you admire and what traits do you admire the most?

3. Do you mimic anyone? If so, who and why?

4. How do people describe you?

5. Do you have a favorite book, movie, story? If so, what is the main message that impacts you the most?

6. What are three things that you must experience with another in a relationship? For example, they have to be honest, playful, and can get serious when needed.

7. Do you have any key things that bother you the most that you would never want to do?

After all the reflecting from above, write some key words which define your core values. Example words may include: health, generosity, responsibility, integrity, respect, authenticity, kindness.

BACK TO SELF

One client reported using it with noticeable improvement whenever he felt ungrounded. See what happens for you.

1. Bring your hands together. Together they represent all of you.

2. Now, have your right hand represent the part of you seeking approval, love and acceptance from others. Move your right hand slowly away from your left hand. As you do this, notice the space between your hands. The left hand is hanging there, representing the part of you that senses something is missing.

3. Now, continue to notice the space between your right hand and your left hand.

4. Consider how it feels to have gone that far away from yourself.

5. Now, slowly see what happens when you move your hands together. Be certain to move slowly.

6. How does it feel to come back to yourself?

7. Journal on your experience.

WASHING YOUR HANDS

1. Write a list of three things you hear yourself say that sound like you learned them from your family/culture. Example:

   a. *Children should be seen and not heard.*

   b. *You made your bed, now you better lie in it.*

   c. *Two wrongs don't make a right.*

2. When did you start hearing this? *These are things I remembered from the time I was very little.*

3. How do you feel when you hear it? *Punished.*

4. Do you live by these statements? *Yes. They come to me without thinking.*

5. Let's now start to wash some of these statements away one at a time.

   a. Choose one situation to start with.

   b. Breathe in and out. Imagine yourself going from your place to a wooded or sandy area. As you start to walk there in your mind's eye, see what it feels like to move from your left foot to your right foot. As you move from side to side, you are going closer to a beautiful area filled with nature sounds. Notice the sounds. Smell the air. Look around. Feel the air touching your skin. Notice something catching your eye. It is a beautiful body of water. You can't help but settle in and stare at it. As you look into the water you relax and feel more and more comfortable. Your mind and body relax. You begin to contemplate the statement you started with. You connect to moments in time when you or another used this statement. You feel various sensations. As you continue to be with what comes up, at a certain point you decide to rest your hands in the water and let the water wash away what is no longer yours to live by. You start to think of new ways to understand and approach situations where you previously acted on automatic pilot. You feel soothed and refreshed. When you are ready, you slowly leave and return to the location you started. At your own speed, slowly open your eyes. Move around and stretch to return to feeling calm, grounded and connected.

c. Journal about your insights.

BALL OF LIGHT: CLEANSING OUR ENERGY

We will now do a visualization of cleansing your energy I call the Ball of Light.

This will help you clear your body's energy for more vitality. We will start with imagining a ball of light at the top of your head and have the ball slowly roll down and clear out your energy.

1. Find a comfortable position. Sitting is ideal for this exercise.

2. Sense a ball of light at the top of your head. This ball of light will slowly grow as it descends and gathers all the negative thoughts, feelings, and sensations that are weighing you down.

3. Imagine the ball of light having a violet light. Notice how bright the violet light is. Have it start to gather particles of busy thoughts, blocked ideas, fears, and worries blocking you from being open-minded and feeling peace around connection. Let all that is not supporting your guidance, wisdom, and inner strength gather onto the ball.

4. Now notice it coming into your forehead in the area between your eyes. Many people call this area the third eye. Notice an indigo light. Let all that is blocking your vision and willingness to see the beauty of life gather on the ball of light. Let all that is blocking you from seeing with greater consciousness and clarity gather on the ball.

5. Now watch it continue to roll into your throat area turning into a blue light. Here all those things that are blocking you from self-expression, speaking your truth, needs, inner voice, and creativity gather onto the ball.

6. The ball continues to roll toward your heart and chest with a green glow to it. Let all that is affecting your heart area gather onto the ball, such as loneliness, resentment, grief or loss.

7. It continues to roll down into your upper stomach area with a yellow light. Let all that is not supporting your

wisdom and intuition gather on to the ball, such as self-doubt, the opinions of others, and ideas of unworthiness.

8. The ball continues to roll into your lower stomach with the color orange. Let all that is negatively impacting your relationships go onto the ball. Watch your thoughts continue to move onto the ball.

9. The ball continues to roll to the base of your spine and takes on the color red. Let all that impacts your self-worth gather onto the ball.

10. See the ball continuing to move down your body out your lower spine and lower legs all the way through the floorboards of the building you are in.

11. Let it roll through the foundation, into the soil and all the layers of the earth, into the waters, all the way to the molten lava. May the fire transform it into clarity and beauty.

CHAPTER 3 EXERCISES

STUCK VISIONS/STUCK BELIEFS

This exercise is ideal if you are feeling stuck in negative beliefs. It can also be used to reframe these beliefs, images or thoughts you have discovered from the content in this chapter.

1. Choose a situation where you feel stuck.
2. Listen to the inner dialogue that goes with it. For example: *I am sitting in my driveway thinking, I never should have moved. I hate this new house.*
3. Imagine the situation as clearly as you can. Rebuild the image in your mind with all your senses, smell what it is like in the car, hear the sounds, notice how the air feels on your skin, look at what is in front of you as if you are there now.
4. What are you thinking? *I hate this new house. I hate myself for saying yes to moving.*
5. What would you like to know instead? This new thought needs to be something you are willing to say yes to. You can't change your past but you can change your relationship to it and how you live, because of your thoughts. A new thought might be:
6. *I am grateful for what brought us here, and I love and appreciate myself for following my decision. I am happy here and appreciate myself for being part of the decision.*
7. Now, imagine yourself in that moment as if it is now. Rebuild it with the new thoughts going through your head but everything else is the same. You are sitting in

the car looking in the same direction seeing the same thing but the end thoughts have changed.

8. Notice how you feel in your body and in that moment.

9. When you are ready to finish, slowly look around your location, breathe deeply and stretch your body. Be aware of the day, the time and the place you are in. Squeeze your arms. Gently rub your head and shoulders. Complete the exercise as you need to.

10. Revisit this new image in your daily meditation practice. Over time it will replace the old.

INTENTION SETTING

Use this approach for any task you are setting out to do, or a thought you want to change or to simply start your day.

For example:

1. State what you want to shift, such as shifting a strong belief you have been carrying which blocks you from getting a certain job: *I am not good enough.*

2. What is the motive to change it, and what is the hesitation/resistance/conflict around changing it? *I feel it has not served me and there is a part of me that is scared to shift because that is the only way I know life—yet I want to and am willing to take steps toward it.*

3. State clearly your intention to shift. *I am willing to change my thinking around not being good enough.*

4. From here you will start to notice this willingness to go from "I am not good enough" to "I am good enough" (or even more, depending on how far you are willing to set your intention and live up to it. Take it step by step.) This

will bring new opportunities to you. Internally, you may experience it as being guided to certain people, places or things. Sometimes your intention may appear blocked, yet your ability to discover where you are stuck is still part of the manifesting process. Working through being stuck can lead to the name of a therapist, healer, coach, or place of worship to support you. Or, you may start to go to the doctor, gym, shift eating patterns, to name a few ways we shake free on the way to manifesting our intentions. All these things can occur because you set your intention and desire in a new direction. Great work, Captain!

RECEIVING POSITIVE COMMENTS

1. Ask people you know care about you to tell you things they like/love about you.
2. Write them on a Post-it.
3. Stick the Post-it around in your house.
4. Each time you pass it, repeat what it says and then move it so every time you walk by it, it is fresh and new. If you don't move it over time you will walk right past it because you saw it there before.
   a. When someone says something nice to you repeat the words to yourself like the most delicious piece of food you ever tasted. Then slowly take it into your entire body imagining it going through your entire digestive track. Release what you do not want, and let the remainder become part of your circulatory system. Receive it into every cell

of your body where you want it. Feel the warmth, the love, the compassion of this statement and the love from the person.

b. Look in the mirror, into your eyes, repeat a phrase or two and see what it is like to receive your own words as if you are speaking to your best friend.

SWITCHING LITTLE VOICES

This is ideal for any thought patterns that no longer serve you. I have separated the meditation process out into a separate exercise because you can also use it to work with any other thoughts where you feel conflict—besides a little voice pulling you away from your positive intention.

A physical exercise that goes along with the releasing your inner "No" is: Becoming Free. www.cynthasis.com/the-curious-voyage-resources/ (Do not do this or any exercise without first checking with your doctor. Adapt all instruction to your physical comfort, and do at your own risk).

1. Think of the little voice that says some version of "No": *I don't want to do this. It's stupid. I can't… I am not capable. How come it has to be like that?*

It may sound much like a child's or adolescent's voice. For example: you are about to start a new exercise program but you think: *Maybe tomorrow* or *what is the point?*

2. Write down the thoughts and any stories you have in relation to it.

3. Notice your energy as you are thinking about it.

4. Is your body getting tense?

5. Scan your body from the top of your head to the tips of your toes and notice any tension. Take note of it.

6. How does the tension manifest? Is there any connection between the tension and the "No" voice? Does it feel like the "No" voice is weighing you down or blocking you from moving? Watch out for the answer to this question being "No". The "No" voice may be very good at helping you think there is nothing wrong with not doing what you set out to do. For example, if you are starting a new exercise program it may tell you this is not the time, because you have too much work to do. Doing work may sound responsible, but it is really just an excuse to not start the new pattern of exercising. You may need to open your mind to discovering things different than you have up to now as you are shaking an established pattern.

7. How is your breathing being affected now as you are doing this process?

8. Notice.

9. Take a moment to do some drawing, move your body or whatever you need to do to feel and hear the negative voices expressing themselves. Sometimes putting on hard drumming music helps to get it moving.

10. Often the "No" voices are a form of fear talking. You can work with it using the *Meditation Using Three Voices* Exercise that follows—or for now, simply notice and journal about it.

MEDITATION USING THREE VOICES

This three-part process connects with aspects of the self, one at a time. It has helped many people overcome confusion, obsessive thinking, worrying, emotional reactions, anxiety and personal/interpersonal conflicts. I was originally introduced to this process through the Pathwork, a self-growth, self-transformation process. This process is on YouTube at: https://youtu.be/7eeEfxdt64o.

1. Find a comfortable spot and set some time aside. It is best to have a journal or paper to write on, because writing creates movement, change and transformation out of our original thought—or the loopy thinking we can get caught in.

2. Notice the part of you that has decided to do this, and even found this tool to explore, is your healthy ego. It is the executor in you that makes decisions, sets time aside, and follows through. It is the part of you that observes, gets curious and wants to know.

   a. Take note that you are asking for help with this thought, conflict, fear and/or "No" voice. I will use the example of wanting to start a new exercise program.

   b. Define the conflict clearly: *I would like help with the part of me that keeps putting off my desire to exercise.*

   c. Notice how you are stuck with the conflict: *I want to, but I never get around to it.*

   d. How has this affected your life? *I am feeling sluggish, falling into old patterns of not wanting to do much, a little depressed, bloated, irritable.*

e. What inner conflicts are you now living with because you may be following a rule from your rulebook that relates to this issue? *The rule in my family has been that work comes first, so now I have no time to exercise. There also has been a rule to be healthy so not sure how I can do both which is making me feel worse about myself. It is a downward spiral. I just want to veg out.*

f. Notice this inner conflict has two opposing forces. Part of you wants something different. *I want to feel better, but I feel overwhelmed with everything I have to do.*

g. The conflict may have been showing up in your life as frustration, anger, depression, anxiety, to name a few ways. *Feeling more depressed and not as good as other people. I am comparing myself more and feeling more lethargic. I don't want to do things I normally think are fun.*

h. However conflict has appeared, think of it as a part of you that has not had a need met, been understood or heard. For this process think of it as a part of you that is younger than your present age. *I am feeling like a young adult who is overwhelmed.*

i. It may want something from the other person, something that is less authentic, honest or straightforward, or it could be that it does not want to follow some rule or requirement (could be it just doesn't want to get out of bed and go to work), feels angry, mad, scared, sad, self-righteous, bullied, or thinks it knows what is best for you and in some way, even thinks it is protecting you. In fact, it may have been very useful at some point, but it is no longer needed as often or in the same way.

j. Take time to hear what this part is: *Frustrated part that is just fed up with life.*

k. Observe its thoughts, feelings and actions: *Sad, lonely, disappointed.*

l. Ask it what it wants: *A vacation.*

m. Ask it what it needs: *Time.*

n. Keep looking at it, observing it and hearing it: *As I keep listening, I hear that it wants alone time and a sense of connection with nature.*

o. Thank it for sharing this information with you: *Thank you, Self, for sharing.*

3. Turn toward your wise inner self/higher power/higher self/inner knowing, and ask for help with this part. It is important to not go into the hard, painful feelings and thoughts without support from the best in you. We all have a higher/best part that is ready, willing and able to assist, when we ask. This can also be the present day, strong, adult self that understands, has compassion and wisdom. We each refer to this part of ourselves in slightly different ways. If you need to, you can ask for support from your God, as you experience God. The key is that this part of you is different than the ego. It has that kind

of intuitive wise knowing that is beyond logical thinking. It can help when you feel stuck.

4. Let a conversation open up between the "unmet need self" and the "wise part". This is not a fix-it conversation, but a willingness to sit and listen and have love toward the part of you that feels its needs are unmet.

5. Wait and see what happens when truth meets pain and confused thinking: *As I kept asking it what it needed, I felt less identified with it and felt like my higher self was the part asking the young adult what she needed. This helped me start to feel more compassion and shifted me away from frustration.*

Let's try this with some of the rules we spoke of earlier. *I am supposed to be with family this weekend, but I don't want to go.*

Key words are: "supposed to." So, if you are in a conflict and you hear "should have," "would have," "could have," or "supposed to" but don't want to, it is helpful to do this process.

1. Decide to take this upsetting decision into the meditation process.

2. State what the issue is. *I don't really want to go, but I know I should.*

3. Listen to that part of you that is saying "no" to going. That part may say: *My values say "go" because it is family, and my feelings say "no" because they are all hypocrites. They lie and cheat each other. They are so fake.* Let that voice that says "no" to going continue to express itself.

4. You may feel overwhelmed on how to resolve this, and that is a good time to turn to the wiser voice.

5. Speak and invite the wiser voice to come in: *I need your help. I hear all these negative thoughts. I feel the anger and am stuck.*

Often the state of stuck is because we feel that "child part" or because we were never allowed to follow our own voice. This wise voice will go beyond the words and further into the feelings. It may ask:

When you realize they are fake and hurtful:

1. *What happens to you?*
2. *What do you want from this?*
3. *What do you need?*
4. *What do you really need?*

At some point the part that does not want to go, calms down and there often is a deep inner connection.

As stated earlier, we can't change others but we can change the way we respond to a situation, or our habitual perspective, and we can soothe our inner parts that were originally wounded. From there we can make wiser choices of how we want to approach the situation.

The above exercise also gives us a deeper understanding of whatever our issue is. It can be used to help us set a new course.

Start Digging Into What You Desire and Your Intention

Desire is a longing for what you truly want.

Intention is what you are willing to put your action behind to bring about your desire.

So, ask yourself these questions:

1. *What games did I enjoy playing?*
2. *How did my playful activities match my desires?*
3. *What do I want?*
4. *What do I need?*
5. *What do I truly desire?*

The other question around desire to consider is: *What percentage of my energy is behind this desire?*

If you respond with less than 80 percent, explore deeper what you really need to help you believe in your desire.

Ask: *What is stopping me from aligning with this desire?*

What am I willing to move, shift, change to help make this desire stronger?

You may want to do some Self-Spotting on this. (See Chapter 1)

Once you have a really strong sense of your desire, move to the following Set Your Intentions Exercise.

Set Your Intentions

This exercise will help you set your course with focus and purpose. Intention is a key ingredient for manifestation. You want to first align with the energy that supports your values so you can create your desire.

1. Think of what it is you would like to create. For example: *I want to expand my business.*

2. How is that in alignment to your values? *I'm shy, so not really.*

3. What are the characteristics you now possess to help you manifest that desire, and what characteristics do you need to strengthen to create this? For example, *I may want to expand my business but I really feel shy and resist networking. I need to first work on my shyness to help strengthen my energy to be in alignment with my intention.*

4. How ready are you to manifest this in your life and set your intention for it to happen? If the answer is 80 percent or more go to Question 6. If it is less, explore questions 3-5.

5. What is stopping you?

6. What next steps do you need to take to help you set the intention?

7. What characteristics do you want to align with to help you get to your desired creation?

8. Can you make the intention different to fit those next steps?

9. Are you having any internal negative self-talk that is making this hard to manifest? For example: *I want to switch my career. Yet, I don't see how that is possible.* What in my rulebook says I can't? Use the exercises in Chapter 2 to help you with these rules.

10. Create a mental image for your desire. See it as an actual scene you are in much like a movie scene. Bring life to it. Imagine it, desire it and expect it is already so.

Below we break down how to work with your imagination and expectations to support your intention.

VISUALIZATION INTO A NEW STATE

This exercise will help you expand into a new way of being. Keep a journal as you articulate your thoughts.

1. Do your own research by observing other people who have aspects you would like to emanate or the life you would like to have. If you can see it in them then there must be some part of you that has it too—otherwise you would probably not notice or be interested in those attributes. A teacher once taught me that we are only jealous of the things we can have for ourself.

2. Once you finish your research and have a sense of what you wish for and can see it more clearly, start to build it.

   a. What is the vibration of the characteristic, the lifestyle? What body posture do you take on when living this way? What color, sound, smell and/or flavor represents it?

   b. What is a day like in that life?

   c. If you enjoy art projects, create something that represents this life.

Vision boards are great outlets to reflect and express. They can take on a power of their own. One time I did a vision board and ended up moving into a house with the same countertop that was on the vision board. I never thought of countertops as a real concern or need. It was a "coincidence." I also noticed over time I got some form of everything on the board.

NIGHTLY GRATITUDE

Make a brief list of what makes you feel grateful. You may need to start with thinking of three people you are grateful for each night to get your mind moving in the right direction. If that is too challenging, start with things instead of people, but research has shown that gratitude journaling tends to be more effective when participants focus on gratitude for people rather than material objects. Take time to savor each blessing, and remain open to surprises.

CLEARING PRIDE, SELF-WILL AND FEAR

This exercise can help you become conscious of how these three primary faults impact a situation and/or relationship. Use it when you feel stuck in a pattern, mood or relationship. Use writing or talking out loud to help you get clarity and shift your thoughts and energy.

1. Pride
   a. What is your pride? How do you wish or see the other person(s) as not as good as you think they should be?
   b. How do you justify yourself in the situation?
   c. What do you think is wrong with the situation or other person(s)?
   d. How could you do this better?
   e. How are you comparing yourself to the situation or other person(s)? Are you better or worse?
   f. Do you feel competitive?

    g. Does that person remind you of someone? Are you better or worse?

2. Self-will

    a. What are your demands or expectations in this situation?

    b. What are you resisting giving up about your position?

    c. What do you keep asking for? When we ask repeatedly or keep trying that is actually a form of control. If you are holding on to control, you may be trying to push your will on the other person(s).

3. Fear

    a. How are you afraid in this situation?

    b. What are you not getting or asking for because fear says not to ask?

    c. What is the dialogue fear is speaking to you?

    d. What is the belief behind your fear statements?

    e. What rule in your rulebook are you acting from?

    f. What value are you afraid to live by because things won't work out the way you want?

You may want to do some journaling or meditating to get to the origin of this pattern. This may need some outside support and help to uncover and release.

CHAPTER 4 EXERCISES

LOVE, POWER, SERENITY EXERCISE: RELEASING CAPES

These inquiry questions can help you explore other situations and shift the energy. They will expand on the Pride, Self-will and Fear Exercise from Chapter 3.

1. First, state the situation. For example, *thinking about what was wrong with the way a loved one is living their life.*

2. Next, what is your intention in order to create the best outcome in the situation? In the example, you may wish to *keep the love and connection open between the two of you.*

3. What belief/rule from your rulebook could you shift to help you align yourself better with your intention? In the example, *I have a belief/rule in the power of judging others and thinking I know what is best for the other person.*

4. Write down what your belief might be, and notice:

    a. Where is my willful demand that I be right, I be heard, I be seen and/or I be understood in this situation? How is it blocking me from having my intention materialize? In the example, *I noticed I was being irritable, short tempered, impatient and closed off.*

    b. In what way may I be trying to force the other person to do things or see things my way? In the example, *I would be overly active in giving my opinion.*

    c. How may I be withholding or withdrawing from the other person? Acts of withholding or withdrawing often indicate there is some kind of power struggle going on in the situation. If so, see what your part is and what you could surrender to create a positive shift. In the example, *I chose to surrender into trust. Not just for my partner, but to the larger idea that whatever happens to us as a couple is what is meant to be.* This is where serenity comes in, and a great tool to use for surrendering is the opening of the Serenity Prayer: *God grant me the serenity to accept the things I cannot change.* (I can't control another person's behavior. Feel free to replace the word 'God' with one that is more comfortable for you if you prefer.) *The courage to change the things I can.* (I stopped myself, became observant and chose to shift my thoughts and actions.)

And the wisdom to know the difference. (I can't control the outcome by trying to get someone to be different.)

5. Visualization: Imagine you are at the edge of a lake. You are wearing three fine capes. They are the capes of pride, self-will and fear.

    a. Cape of pride: This cape is designed with all the ways you are right and ways you are better or worse than the other.

    b. Cape of self-will: It is sewn with all the ways you are forcing something in the situation so your way can win.

c. Cape of fear: This cape is filled with all the statements that make you think you can't let go of your position. It knows all the ways the other person is wrong and you are right. It is filled with beliefs about how you are better or worse and has you convinced this is the way it is and if you shift in any direction something bad will happen. You can't let go. Yet you long for your intention to set you free.

Freeing yourself into the lake of the unknown: As you imagine yourself standing there wearing these capes and looking into the water think of what you desire and long for. What is your intention? What do you imagine is possible for you? And, when you are ready, take off the capes one at a time and dive into the lake of the unknown and let your intuition and imagination show you the way.

The above is one of many ways to let go of our tight dualistic thinking.

DANCING INTO LOVE

Another fun way to work with our energy is to dance it out. The dance described in this section can be done sitting or standing—whatever you are capable of doing. You can use your mind to imagine it. Visualization and movement have been found to help people heal from physical restrictions. It works similar parts of the brain.

Dance in whatever way is physically right for you. You may need to simply imagine the action of dancing or move your arms or feet and sway based on your physical ability.

1. Find a place that is private or comfortable for you to feel free to move.

2. Set an intention of what you want to dance toward. You may state something like:

   a. My intention is to release my judgments toward _____ and to open my heart to compassion.

   b. Or, my intention is to release the tension in my body that is blocking my peace in relation to _____. Or, my intention is to open to all possibilities to find _____. Choose something that has meaning to you.

   c. Turn on some drumming music. Various versions are found on YouTube, or choose a strong rhythmic beat that suits you. Let the beat impact your energy.

3. Start to move. See what happens.

4. Shift the music to other rhythms. Gabrielle Roth speaks of 5 rhythms in her movement video called The Wave, A Moving Meditation:

   a. Flowing (fluid movements)

   b. Staccato (short stops and starts)

   c. Chaos (wild and free)

   d. Lyrical (playful and light and will move to)

   e. Stillness (the still point of your moving center)

5. Create your own. Find a playlist that suits you. Notice how you feel now that you have moved your body.

Dance, movement (imagined or actual) and integrating our body into our awareness will shift us to a deeper connection to self.

Dance up your inner family and shift internal relations.

You can do this by putting on some music that has a masculine tone, a feminine tone, a playful tone and then dancing the integration of the masculine/father energy, the feminine/mother energy and the playful child energy. Let the inner family integrate, shift, move, heal and fall in love with each other.

BRAIN/BODY CONNECTION POWER

A basic point of entry, exit and regulation is our brainstem. Here we have parts of our brain that support our respiration, circulation, balance, digestion and much more. It is a pathway for our nerves to go from our brain to our body and back again.

Connecting the two:
1. Get comfortable in a seated position.
2. Place one hand gently on top of your head and the other at the base of your skull and neck.
3. Breathe and notice.
4. Let your eyes gaze at a spot or close your eyes and follow your breath and rhythm.
5. Notice what happens. Switch hands when ready.
6. Take a deep breath and notice how you feel.

BREATH TO CONNECT LOVE AND POWER

This exercise will open up your body and support the connection between love and power. Perform these movements based on your physical ability. Imagine, sit or lie down. Do not continue if you are finding the breath creating anxiety versus joy. Sometimes full breathing can present a nervousness and activate old pain you are needing to approach with professional help. If this happens seek help to work with breath in a therapeutic environment.

1. Put one hand on your heart and one on your lower belly. If you are lying down bend your knees.
2. Breathe in and feel the air going into your lower belly pushing your lower hand up then your upper hand. Let your head stretch back and your chest expand.
3. Gently press (so you are aware you are releasing first from your chest then your lower belly) with your upper hand as you breathe out. Curl your shoulders with your head tucked in. Suck in with your lower belly as you continue to exhale.
4. Wait until ready to take the next breath and do it again.
5. Each time feeling your hands.
6. Now breathe in again expanding your chest and exhale contracting.
7. If you feel a lot of excitement tap, stamp or shake your legs to release the energy.
8. Let out a sigh or any other sound to open your chest.
9. Keep breathing and bring your awareness into your heart, lower belly and back sensing you are connected within. Feel strong, vital and loved.

Compassion

This exercise is ideal to pause and connect to a state of love.

1. Breathe deeply with one or two hands on your heart.
2. Think and/or feel compassion for yourself.
3. Speak out loud 3 times: *I am safe. I am kind. I am whole. I am love.*
4. Now think of someone you love, and state 3 times: *You are safe. You are kind. You are whole. You are love.*
5. Now think of someone you are challenged by. Speak out loud 3 times: *You are safe. You are kind. You are whole. You are love.*
6. Now think of your community. Speak out loud 3 times: *We are safe. We are kind. We are whole. We are love.*
7. Now think of the world. *We are safe. We are kind. We are whole. We are love.*

There are various exercises on developing compassion as it is a state of being to develop.

https://zenhabits.net/a-guide-to-cultivating-compassion-in-your-life-with-7-practices/

CHAPTER 5 EXERCISE

Listening

Practice listening and being. This will help you develop a different way of being with sound and vibrations for increasing your intuition.

1. Find a comfortable position to be for the next five minutes.
2. Gently close your eyes.

3. Notice the sounds around you.
4. Wait, and simply notice.
5. As thoughts arise, see them going past, like waves. Do not grab onto any thought, and if you do, simply come back to listening.
6. Notice the sounds outside you.
7. Pick one and observe it much like you were listening to a song. When your mind wanders pick another sound and do the same.
8. After three sounds chose to notice your sounds. Notice your breath.
9. Listen to any other sounds you experience within.
10. Simply listen and when you feel ready simply open your eyes.

In this space of conscious listening, notice what it is like to receive and listen to others without an agenda and without needing to add anything but your presence.

ABOUT THE AUTHOR

Cynthia Schwartzberg, LSCW, is a well-recognized leader in the groundbreaking Brainspotting field. She has spent decades using Brainspotting and other highly regarded techniques to help individuals and couples discover their authentic selves and lead richer, freer and more meaningful lives.

Cynthia is currently a practicing therapist in Atlanta who delights in the voyage of authenticity she and her clients embark on daily. Using the latest in neuroscience as well as ancient wisdom traditions from around the world, she has devoted her life to going as far as possible into the experiences of both curiosity and wonder.

For more information or to order more books, please visit:

https://www.cynthasis.com/the-curious-voyage/

Made in the USA
Columbia, SC
16 December 2023

28665222R00114